Praise for M̶

"As a marketer, your success rises and falls on your ability to apply actions that actually impact your business, and truly drive revenue. That's what's great about this book--it's loaded with actionable, applicable takeaways that you can immediately apply to your business and get results with. Highly recommended!"

MARCUS SHERIDAN
Author, *They Ask You Answer*

"The best way to learn is from those who are doing it. David's new book takes this sentiment to the next level by featuring experts from around the world who give practical advice on how to succeed in today's digital marketplace. If you're looking for an up-to-date digital marketing read, then this is your guide."

JUSTIN CHAMPION
Principal Inbound Professor, *HubSpot*

"This book is packed full of awesome, actionable tips from the top minds in the industry. It's easy to read, so you can grab the tips and get right to work. Every business owner and marketer should read it immediately!"

GREG GIFFORD
Vice President of Search, *Wikimotive*

"Comprehensive, timely and actionable, if you're a marketer or a business owner who wants to be cutting edge in your approach, read Marketing Now."

LARRY KIM
Founder, *WordStream* & CEO, *MobileMonkey*

"David has produced an awesome book of gold! It's bang up to date and relevant with some of the best industry insider tips in the world. If you truly want to stay ahead of the curve, reading this book is going to help you achieve that goal."

PATRICK CUTLIFFE
Founder, *BuzzStart Academy*

"If becoming a successful online marketer is on your roadmap, get yourself a copy of this book."

ISAAC RUDANSKY
CEO, *AdVenture Media Group*

"David has assembled the ultimate compilation from the very, very best marketers on the planet."

DENNIS YU
CEO, *BlitzMetrics*

"An amazing collection of smart people sharing their best tips. To be able to bring them all together in one book is an achievement. This book will pay for itself over and over again."

JIM BANKS
CEO, *Spades Media*

"I love the tremendous work David Bain and his team has put in to this project. Get to the point, hands-on advice in all digital marketing aspects from highly experienced practitioners facing the same challenges you do."

KRISTIAN HAANES
Founder, *Webinara*

"This book is filled with actionable and helpful quotes from some of the most well-respected marketers on the planet. What's not to love?"

ALEXANDER ROYLE
Head of Audience, *BBC Studios*

"The event that produced the book was a whirlwind of amazing advice from brilliant marketers (and a lot of fun too). The book is an impressive representation of that – a stunning resource that is enjoyable to read. And because of the way it is organised, easy to dip in and out of, making it perfect as travel reading!"

JASON BARNARD
Founder, *Kalicube*

"An absolute must-read if you want to stay ahead of the digital marketing curve!"

JONNY ROSS
Founder, *Fleek Marketing*

"A fantastic, actionable book full of bite-sized advice from the best in the business."

AARON LEVY
Group Director, SEM, *Tinuiti*

"This book is packed full of the best tips and strategies by the world's experts in their field!"

TERESA HEATH-WAREING
Director, *THW Marketing*

"An impressive collection of actionable advice from most of the world's digital marketing experts!"

DAVID SZETELA
CEO, *FMB Media*

"Marketing Now is the leading source of information for staying on top of changes in the marketing industry."

MICHAEL FLEISCHNER
Founder, *Big Fin Solutions*

"Digital marketing requires a grasp of both technical and human skills alongside and increasing amount of up to date digital psychology and legal knowledge. No one can be an expert in every area drawing from the wealth of knowledge of industry specialists is really the only way to keep up with the speed of change. Marketing Now has done a great job at vetting experts to help support this end."

LEXI MILLS
Ceo, *Shift6*

"Marketing Now is full of advice from experienced marketers that will help you today, and help you see where marketing is going in the future, so you can ensure you are on top of the ever changing landscape."

BRAD GEDDES
Co-Founder, *Adalysis*

"There aren't many places where you can find the 'favourite' marketing tactics of top marketers around, but here David's managed to put together not just a dozen, but hundreds! Ace advice, all the way through. Put even 10% of it into action and you'll see big results."

COLIN GRAY
Founder, *The Podcast Host*

"Digital marketing continues to evolve and there's no better place to stay up to date than the books that David produces!"

MARK ASQUITH
CEO, *Rebel Base Media*

"If you ever feel stalled in your marketing, if you're ever looking for a fresh approach, scanning a chapter of this book can be like a trip to a digital marketing spa."

MARK TRAPHAGEN
VP of Content Strategy, *Aimclear*

"This book is such a brilliant idea! It gives you a real insight into what's happening now in the marketing world, from the experts themselves. It's full of great advice and is a must-read for anyone interested in marketing"

LEAH BUCKINGHAM-WARNER
Founder, *Leah Buckingham Digital Marketing*

"Fabulous, easily digestible tips and ideas to enhance your marketing"

KATY HOWELL
CEO, *Immediate Future*

"Marketing Now is filled with timeless advice that will help you gain an edge in your market. David Bain has interviewed hundreds of marketers who have years of experience in the digital space. He distilled all of that knowledge into the most actionable high-profit tips. I would highly recommend this book to any business that wants to grow."

ANDREA VAHL
Founder, *AndreaVahl.com*

"How many places will you get this many digital marketing tips in one place? Read it and get inside the minds of the leading industry professionals."

HANNAH BUTCHER
Head of Content, *Koozai*

"Marketing Now is packed full of useful (and current) digital marketing tips and tricks. I encourage anyone who is looking to improve their marketing to read it!"

TOM TREANOR
Global Head of Marketing, *Arm Treasure Data*

"What marketing professionals want is hands-on information they can use right away. This excellent piece of content is just that."

BAS VAN DEN BELD
Digital Marketing Consultant, *BasVanDenBeld.com*

"Marketing Now is a must-read for anyone who is in digital marketing or is looking to enter the industry."

PAUL LOVELL
Founder, *Always Evolving SEO*

"This is a must read featuring top tips from industry leading experts in digital marketing!"

LAURIE WANG
Founder, *LaurieWang.com*

"It's amazing to have this compendium of digital marketing knowledge. So much of the advice here is timeless, and will be as useful to marketers ten years from now as it is right now."

ARIANNE DONOGHUE
Associate Director, *Edit*

"When it comes to content marketing, David, pulls no punches. He literally gets in every nook and cranny with this book. This is a must read for marketers working with content."

CHAD POLLITT
VP of Marketing, *inPowered*

"David is a great friend and inspiration. He has taught me a great deal about how to produce professional quality podcasts and webinars. He has put a lot of effort into producing this book and I have no doubt that you will take significant value from it."

LUKASZ ZELEZNY
Founder, *SEO London*

"The best way to learn is from experience, the best way to fast-track that learning is to learn from everyone else's experiences. That's what this book does, combining a range of specialists with proven results and learnings, provided in a fun to read way, to help provide key takeaways you can apply to your own strategies."

KEVIN GIBBONS
Founder, *Re:signal*

"David's done a wicked job of collating such a vast array of useful information into this bite-sized, well-written book."

DAN KNOWLTON
Co-Founder, *Knowlton Marketing*

"The book you should read to keep up with upcoming digital marketing trends!"

ALEYDA SOLIS
Founder, *Orainti*

"If you're looking for up-to-the-minute, but easy-to-implement social media marketing tips and advice then you absolutely have to have this book. Every single contributor offers a really simple, but powerful idea that could really ramp up your results! I can't believe the amount of actionable value in this book!"

JULIA BRAMBLE
Founder, *BrambleBuzz*

"Great up-to-date advice for any marketer this year!"

AJ WILCOX
Founder, *B2Linked*

"Marketing Now is an amazing resource. Packed full of great advice that every marketer should know. I've certainly learnt a lot from it!"

STEVE LINNEY
Marketing Manager, *The Security Bureau*

"This amazing piece is full of incredible insights that not only inspire, they make you want to take action now. Great stuff."

MICHAEL BONFILS
Managing Director, *SEM International*

"I love David Bain's perspective on online marketing. His approach of thoughtfully curating and speaking to many, many qualified experts in their field is really unique and enlightening."

PHIL PALLEN
Brand Strategist, *Phil Pallen Collective*

"David has done it again! Producing a book jam-packed with expert advice across the world of marketing. If you want to get bang up to date with what's happening in the world of marketing, this book is for you."

IAN ANDERSON GRAY
Founder, *iag.me*

"Maybe the most complete collection of ideas and recommendations about modern marketing you can find nowadays."

GIANLUCA FIORELLI
Founder, *iLoveSEO.net*

"You won't very often find as much knowledge in one place – this is your chance, snap it up while you can!"

CHRIS GREEN
Head of Search, *StrategiQ Marketing*

"Love that there are real world examples and case studies included in the book. Many takeaways and nuggets to help anyone in marketing can be found in this book."

MAT SILTALA
Co-Founder, *Business Of Digital*

"David has put together one of the most comprehensive groups of experts I've seen in the area of digital marketing. The book has an immense amount of knowledge and tips from the pros to share."

JOE GRIFFIN
Co-Founder, *ClearVoice*

"David is a true master in our industry! His constant advice over the years has helped many business and digital marketing professionals."

MARK WRIGHT
Winner, *UK Apprentice TV Show* and Founder,
Climb Online

"Great tips from great experts! David is one of the most connected people in digital marketing today and he has harnessed those connections to their fullest."

DIXON JONES
Marketing Director, *Majestic.com*

"If you're looking for tactical tips with the latest advice from true experts, this book is what you need!"

ASHLEY SEGURA
Director of Marketing, *Madhouse Matters*

"This book is packed with practical and strategic advice for marketers to get better results from digital. If you are ready to take your results to the next level, this is a must-read featuring great advice from some of the smartest marketers in the industry."

KRISTA NEHER
Author, *Visual Social Marketing for Dummies*
and CEO, *Boot Camp Digital*

"Creating this book was an excellent way to document the great tips that all of the renowned experts gave in this awesome event. Many people love to read books, but it's so difficult to get digital marketing advice that is fully up-to-date in book format. Readers can be sure that this particular book is giving them information that is relevant as of now!"

PAM AUNGST
President and Founder, *Pam Ann Marketing*

marketing now

134 of the World's Leading SEO, Online Advertising and Social Media Gurus Share Their Number 1, Actionable Digital Marketing Tip, Helping You to Grow Your Website Visitors, Boost Your Ecommerce Conversion Rates and Accelerate Your Online Business

DAVID BAIN

Copyright © 2019 Purple Internet Marketing Limited SC306577

All rights reserved.

ISBN-13: 978-1-64085-924-1 (Hardback)
ISBN-13: 978-1-64085-923-4 (Paperback)

To Noah

CONTENTS

ACKNOWLEDGMENTS

A big thanks to my Marketing Now co-hosts:

- Justin Champion and Courtney Sembler from *Academy. HubSpot.com*
- Mark Asquith from *RebelBaseMedia.io*
- Pam Ann Aungst from *PamAnnMarketing.com*
- Kamila Gornia from *KamilaGornia.com*
- Ian Anderson Gray from *Iag.me*
- Rebekah Radice from *RebekahRadice.com*
- Laurie Wang from *LaurieWang.com*

And a special thanks to the Marketing Now publishing partners:

- HubSpot Academy (*Academy.HubSpot.com*)
- Buzzsumo (*Buzzsumo.com*)
- SEMrush (*SEMrush.com*)
- Mobile Monkey (*MobileMonkey.com*)
- AVADO (*AVADOlearning.com*)

OPENING THOUGHTS

At times it's important to be resolute, to stick to your guns no matter what the crowd says. However, some people's opinions are worthwhile listening to. The challenge is to determine who to listen to, and who to ignore.

Back in early 2017 I published the book 'Digital Marketing in 2017' and I asked my friend and esteemed podcasting pro Mark Asquith to write the foreword – and a wonderful job he did too.

However, one thing he said hit me, "Here we stand today. Digital marketing in 2017 is now simply 'marketing'."

To be honest with you, I'm not sure that I completely agreed with Mark at the time. My background was largely in digital marketing and in my experience, large swathes of more traditional marketers just didn't 'get' digital. And many digital marketers were able to out-perform their more traditional counterparts when it came to driving targeted customers.

Maybe what Mark said was true at the time and maybe it wasn't, but there certainly has been a great deal of change in the digital marketing landscape since. 2017 was the last year that digital marketers were given 'free rein'. Facebook advertising was in its relative infancy and both Cambridge Analytica and GDPR still hadn't happened.

Also, in the years since I published Digital Marketing in 2017, I've had the opportunity to develop digital marketing training programmes for a few very large organisations. In doing so, I've gained a much better understanding of marketing models in general.

As a digital marketer it's easy to get distracted by shiny new things and led by technology. Perhaps that was valuable when traffic was cheap and there was a lot of sense in jumping on a trend quickly, riding it out until something better came along.

But technologies are growing up. As I write this, Google is over 20 years old and Amazon is over 25 years old. They've both learned to put incredible customer experience at the heart of everything they do and it's time for all digital marketers to start doing the same. Now is the time for digital marketers to embrace great, conventional marketing too. Yes, I've changed my thinking. Digital marketing is now simply marketing – it's Marketing Now.

However, I wasn't quite there with my thinking six months ago. In fact, this book was originally going to be called 'Digital Marketing in 2019'. Perhaps a smart move if it was going to be published in late 2018, but not so smart for a book that's due to be published in late 2019!

So what should I call it? 'Digital Marketing in 2020' or something else? I had Mark's sage advice ringing in my ears about the direction that digital marketing was taking. I also had the counsel of book publisher Kary Oberbrunner and entrepreneur coach Chris Ducker, both telling me to be very careful about selecting a book title that could age it's perceived value very quickly.

I re-read the tips shared by all 134 contributors and I realised that the advice shared in this book isn't intended for 2019, or for 2020 for that matter. It's simply advice on how to blend best practice digital marketing with best practice conventional marketing, and do it in a manner that works for the long-term.

None of the tips shared here are short-term wins that won't work next year. This is a book for marketing now and it's also a book for marketing over many years to come.

I'm not sure if Mark had more foresight than me, or if he was a little ahead of his time. Either way, because of things like Cambridge Analytica and GDPR, because of the rising costs and general increased acceptance of digital advertising – and because of the increased awareness of customer journeys and traditional marketing models that still work now – digital marketing has become marketing, marketing now.

I produced Marketing Now in a similar way to my previous book, in that I invited over 100 world-class modern marketers to join me on a livestream series, all sharing their actionable advice.

The breadth and quality of the tips shared were outstanding. Perhaps not surprising though, when you give over 100 of the world's smartest marketing minds three minutes each to share their number one piece of actionable advice.

Even though the tips shared were superb, this book would be a bit of a hard slog to read if it were simply a transcript of the livestream series. It's definitely not that! Every piece of advice has been edited to improve its readability without changing its intended meaning. I've also categorised all of the tips, then added context around them so that they flow neatly together. This was much more work than writing a book from scratch I'm sure!

Use this book as the starting point to create a brand new framework for all of your marketing activities. It isn't designed to go into incredible depth about each topic, but to introduce you to each subject, the importance of it as part of your marketing mix, and to give you the motivation to find out more about it elsewhere.

To make the most of this book, sign up for our 3 free livestreamed or recorded (depending when you watch) implementation workshops at *DavidBain.com/MarketingNow*. Bon voyage!

David Bain
DavidBain.com
December 2019

FOREWORD

The online marketing summits that David Bain puts so much effort into creating have become quite the tradition – with a fantastic selection of speakers sharing their best advice, strategies, tips and tricks.

I have a 'pro tip' for anyone looking to appear on David's next online summit… A couple of years ago, I appeared in his end-of-year recap – calmly waiting for my 3-minute slot with microphone muted and camera turned off – whilst working from home…

Once it was my turn, I switched the microphone and camera on, and started to try and sound clever by sharing my best tip to the audience. Shortly into this, to my horror I noticed that behind me was my washing hanging out to dry! Luckily for you, you're reading the book, so you don't have to see my laundry in the background!

"You can't connect the dots looking forward; you can only connect them looking backwards. So you have to trust that the

dots will somehow connect in your future. You have to trust in something - your gut, destiny, life, karma, whatever."— Steve Jobs

This is one of my favourite quotes, as I've always found in terms of predicting what's coming next, you have to look at the past and then base it on your experience to take a leap of faith on what's coming next.

I've been involved in digital marketing since 2003, and during that time I've found that the main objectives are always the same. Back then, the strategy was to target potential customers who can help you make more money. Today, that hasn't changed at all.

However, the tactics, algorithms and marketplaces have matured since then, and this book introduces, explains and categorises best-practice in a way that will greatly appeal to today's modern marketer.

Marketing Now teaches you about a number of different areas, from SEO, to paid search, to social media, analytics, digital PR and more, as well as marketing models which can be used to overlay the cutting-edge tactics shared.

I always find that to have a solid marketing plan, you need to be well prepared in three clear areas; and the way that David has divided this book into three key sections happens to very closely resemble the way that we structure our campaigns in our own agency.

Here are the tips and subjects that stand out for me:

1) Technical Success

- **Be better locally** – Greg Gifford shares how to maximise Google My Business by fully completing your profile, uploading high quality photography, contributing to Q&A, plus paying attention to how posts look on phone screens.

- **Be prepared for voice search** – a number of experts share how voice is on their marketing agenda, with tips around multilingual campaigns, how writing will be substituted by voice and the fact that Google and Amazon are heavily pushing voice services, expanding to conversational experiences instead of just providing one-off answers.
- **Create an emotional response and reaction from your customers** – Stewart Rogers provides an example where BrewDog had at least 45 swear words in their press release to stand out of the crowd!

2) Creative Success

To have a real impact, you need to get your brand noticed, and the experts provided some real gems to help you do this.

- **Create thumb-stopping content** – it's fiercely competitive to capture social attention, you need to find a way to make people stop and pay attention, says Katy Howell.
- **Live video is dominating content on social media and beyond** - Live video has really dominated the social and content space recently and with good reason says Rebekah Radice.

3) Promotional Success

- **Personalisation at scale** – Purna Virji shares hugely valuable insights on segmenting and targeting your audience. Personalization is key in marketing now.

Our expectations for consumers are changing very fast and we now have a great variety of tools to match the customer needs plus necessary targeting to improve experiences.

- **Invest in your personal brand** – marketers shouldn't be hiding behind the brands and companies they work for – you are missing out on a great deal of attention if you do so – invest in your staff and their training says Joe Apfelbaum.
- **Go and be your audience** – if you're going to be marketing a brand, buy their products and visit their stores so that you can relate to the customer says Lexi Mills.

In my view, the more you know about a range of topics, the more you can discover what really works for you. However, the trick then is to find those one or two big things you can focus on to really move the needle, then you build outwards. Marketing Now will help you to achieve this over the coming year and beyond.

Kevin Gibbons
Resignal.com
December 2019

PART 1:
TECHNICAL SUCCESS

1

GETTING STARTED & BEST PRACTICE

We begin our foray into Marketing Now by considering what to keep from our current activities before ushering in the new – because keeping what currently works and making it better lays solid groundwork for the road ahead.

1) Start off by looking back at last year – Chris Smith

First up is Chris Smith, author of the Conversion Code and Co-Founder of *Curaytor.com*. What does Chris share as his number one piece of actionable advice for Marketing Now?

Chris says: "We often look at the next new thing when we should be reviewing what we did the previous year and making it better this time around.

"I'm a big fan of going back to what you did, and doing it better. One of my favourite sayings is, 'Quit tripping over nickels to pick up pennies.' That's what a lot of marketers do. We can't wait to try something new, because it means we don't have to go back and do a better job of the things that we've done in the past.

"In my business, every year we revisit what we've done in the past, and this process helps us generate thousands of additional leads over the coming year.

"Go into your Google Analytics, and sort out your top performing content by page views, per visitor or by time on site.

"What we've learned is that the content on our site each year that performs the best – when it's not a lead magnet – is incredibly useful next year as a lead magnet.

"We take our top five articles from the prior year and we put them behind a landing page. The fact that they were popular, the fact that our analytics backs-up the fact that our website visitors really enjoyed reading those articles – they stuck around – it almost guarantees that it will work as a lead magnet. That's the first thing we do, we identify the top performing content and we don't let it die a slow death. We recycle it as a landing page and an opt-in lead magnet.

> *"Go into your Google Analytics, and sort out your top performing content by page views, per visitor or by time on site."*
> **CHRIS SMITH**
> *@Chris_Smth*

"The next thing we do is go to our Facebook Page Insights, and do the same thing. We what our most popular five or six posts from the past year were, and then use those to target new people this year.

"As an example, if I have a post that went viral last year and got tons of engagement and really great click-through-rates, a new person that engages with my Facebook Page this year should see that content via a retargeting ad. Use Facebook tracking pixels on your website to make sure that your best content on Facebook gets seen by new visitors.

"The overarching theme of my tip is to go and make what's old new again. Make sure there's not a little bit more juice left in that orange!"

2) Keep chasing perfection – Jono Alderson

For Jono Alderson, Head of Special Ops at *Yoast.com*, looking back at how you did in the previous year is also key to forecasting your success in the future.

Jono says: "Essentially, the secret to modern marketing success is to have a fast, easily usable, technically flawless website with excellent content that truly helps your users. That's not new, and it's not particularly the most current tip, but that remains the way you win. My number one tip is to chase perfection – and not to be afraid of doing so.

"A lot of brands work on the premise of, 'What's the least that we can get away with? How do we do enough to beat this competitor and leapfrog them today?' Actually, the people who really win are the people who say, 'What does the stretch goal look like? What does having the best content on the internet or the most technically perfect website, or the fastest website look like?' Picking at these areas, and really going for it is how you truly win.

"There's a new flavour to this though, and it's something that we've all been overlooking for a long time in digital. This is the year of the brand.

"We've all been caught up on it being the year of mobile, or the year of voice, or AI or blockchain, and this has distracted us from the most important thing – you're never going to rank well or get loads of conversions or shares or whatever metric it is you're after if your product or service sucks.

"This is about getting the basics right. And then, going beyond that and aiming for perfection – whether it's product-market fit or customer service or differentiated features. Having those kinds of goals are what gets you more links, more shares, more visits, more sales – whatever you need.

"Aim to sort your brand out over the coming few months. Take a step away from the website and look at every touchpoint in a consumer's lifespan, from the emails you send to the call centre scripts, the product packaging and the training your quality control teams get – every single aspect of the business.

> *"It's time to put down digital and talk to everyone else about what they do and how that impacts you."*
> **JONO ALDERSON**
> *@jonoalderson*

"Teach them about digital and teach them that the work that they do, the way that they interact with consumers, what they write and their choices of materials or price positioning – all of those things impact digital. Whether it's the speed of your website, how well you rank, or how well your trials integrate, everyone in your business needs to understand that it's all connected. It's time to put down digital and talk to everyone else about what they do and how that impacts you."

3) Focus is what drives results - don't try to do everything yourself – Garrett Moon

Garrett Moon, CEO and Co-Founder of *CoSchedule.com*, thinks that successful modern marketing is all about getting your priorities right.

Garrett says: "I really encourage teams to think about the scope or breadth of the digital marketing that they're doing. I think that as marketers, every year there's more and more channels. And as you try to do more and more, it all becomes very difficult to implement everything to a high standard.

"One of the things that our marketing team consistently does, is we take a look at the projects that we're currently working on: where we're publishing our content, how we prioritize what we do and how we then remove things from our to-do list.

"What we really love to do is to try to find the 10x opportunities, versus the ten percent improvements that can often take up too much of your time.

"Find the 10x opportunities, versus the ten percent improvements that can often take up too much of your time."
GARRETT MOON
@garrett_moon

"We then say, 'What are our goals for the coming year, and what strategies are we going to use to accomplish these goals?' I.e. are we going to use video, how are we going to utilize SEO and how are we going to utilize publishing to different social channels?

"Put each one of your intended strategies up on a Post-it Note, hang it on a whiteboard and start to catalogue them. I like to use a simple one, two, three system to determine how complicated or how much time each of those strategies would take.

"Mark it if a one if it would take a week or less, two if it would take a couple of weeks, and a three if it might take three weeks or longer to execute.

"Start to catalogue your strategies and look at how long they're taking. You must understand that as a marketing team, your time is your absolute, most finite, most difficult to come-by resource. It's not just marketing budget, it's your time.

"Catalogue your strategies by their complexity, then catalogue them by their impact. How much impact could they potentially make to your marketing and to your results over the coming year? Is it a ten percent impact, meaning that they will definitely improve your marketing?

"For example, updating Instagram one more time every day will definitely do a better job of marketing your brand than one less time. But is that really going to give you a significant result or is it going to give you a ten percent incremental result?

"Then, compare those current opportunities to projects that may have the potential to multiply your results by ten. Could you take your number of email subscribers from 5,000 to 50,000 in a year's time by using a certain strategy? And if so, you should make sure that you prioritize this and put it at the top of your list, even if it's a very complex project. In doing so you'd then deprioritize some of the smaller items.

"The beginning of the year is a great time to do it, but even reviewing it once a quarter, or every few months really helps you to stay focused – and focus is what drives the results rather than the breadth of making sure that you're involved in every channel."

Should a marketing team focus on the 10x activities versus ten percent activities regardless of how long they might take you?

Garrett says: "You want to be careful here. If it's a 10x activity and it's classified as a 'level three', it's going to take you a long time. You should probably just focus on one or two of those bigger projects per quarter and you should tackle them as a team.

"It's probably not a good idea to be doing five 'level three' projects all at the same time. Block out how long each of these longer projects should take, and what can be accomplished in your allotted time, depending on how big your team is.

"The most important thing here is using that process to get your team to consistently ask the question – before they dive into a new campaign or project, 'Is this a 10x opportunity, or am I working on a ten percent improvement, and if I'm working on a ten percent improvement, is it at the sacrifice of a 10x opportunity?'"

4) All awesome things are basic things, done exceptionally well – Olga Andrienko

How do you do a better job of focusing on the 10x opportunities that Garrett highlighted in the previous tip if you work in a larger marketing department? Olga Andrienko, Head of Global Marketing at *SEMrush.com* would like to see more data shared between her marketing teams.

> *"All awesome things are basic things, done exceptionally well."*
> **OLGA ANDRIENKO**
> *@Olgandrienko*

Olga says: "What I've realized is that all awesome things are basic things, done exceptionally well. Don't dream about awesome campaigns – ensure that you have everything set up properly on social media, on your blog, and on your website to deliver all of your messaging, smoothly and coherently.

"Once you go into the small details and elements to implement your plans at an excellent level, you outrun 90% of everyone else.

"Something else we discovered recently, working with Forrester is that most marketing teams are not really ready for cross-channel marketing efforts, because they're not sharing data effectively.

"Get your advertising, PR and SEO teams to share their data between one-another. We discovered that just 26% of SEO teams get data from advertising and PR – which is an insanely low number!

"If you work in a specialist marketing team, make sure that other specialist teams have the same information that you do – and then make sure that you align efforts within your company or your marketing team to help you achieve your big goals."

5) Focus on the consumer first - and remember, people love to be helped – Kath Pay

Next up we have Kath Pay – Kath has 19 years of email marketing experience and is Founder of *HolisticEmailMarketing.com*. Kath begun her tip by expressing her concern about how as marketers we tend to be too technology-led.

Kath said: "As email marketers we tend to be very, very led by technology. There's amazing technology out there, and it's really easy to get carried away with all the wonderful things that you can do, but what we really should be doing is focusing on the consumer.

"We've recently done some research and found that consumers (this is not going to come as any surprise!) love customer service. Therefore, when you package up all of your emails as customer service, the customer loves it; they engage more, they open more, they click more and they convert more.

"Go back to basics – it's the fundamentals of human nature. Think about why someone subscribed with you in the first place. Why have they come to your website? Why have they completed the subscribe form, signed up for your newsletter or signed up to receive your alerts? It's because they want something from you.

"It's because you've promised them something and you've set expectations. You might not have committed to any particular frequency, but you've committed to sending them something and what you've committed to send them has become even become more prominent with GDPR. That's one of the central things within GDPR – you have to be transparent and you have to explicitly say what it is that you're going to be delivering to your subscribers.

"When you package up all of your emails as customer service, the customer loves it."
KATH PAY
@kathpay

"For the people on your list, ask yourself, 'What did I first promise them?' It's as simple as that. Start thinking about how you can deliver upon that promise. It's no different to communicating with someone who's made a purchase from you. Pretend you own an e-commerce site and you sold a customer a pair of jeans. You then deliver them a transactional email saying that they'll be receiving their jeans on X date. After that they'll receive their product delivered to their door.

"The promise you deliver on as an e-commerce merchant is no different than the promise you make with email. If someone signs-up to receive an email newsletter, you made a promise that the customer bought into – a transaction took place, even though no money has changed hands (as far as a free newsletter goes). When you're sending email, all you're doing is delivering upon that initial free transaction.

"The core of a transactional email is customer-service oriented. It should be helpful. This also brings us to another point – subscribers are on your list because they have a need, and they like you. They like your products, your services, they read your blog. There's something about what you do that they think is going to help them in their lives. And that's all you need to do. You just need to help your subscribers help themselves. And by doing that, you'll benefit too.

"Emails are a push channel, a very powerful push channel. We therefore tend to be very brand-centric, saying 'Let me tell you about our offers and our specials – all about us, the brand'. Instead, we should be thinking 'How can I help my consumer, who signed up to me, to receive that promise which I made? How can I help them to achieve their objectives?'

"You should be walking around with your subscribers virtually, holding their hand, saying 'what is it that you'd like to achieve and how can I help you do that?' If you help your subscribers to achieve their objectives, by default you'll achieve your objectives too.

"In essence, it's really simple. It's just a case of going back to the grassroots of human nature – people love to be helped."

6) Plan your customer journey – Edwin Raymond

Customers are also at the centre of digital marketing success for Edwin Raymond, Founder of *FloodlightNewMarketing.co.uk*.

Edwin says "I think that successful modern marketing comes down to planning and execution. A lot of marketers correctly speak about customers, how to make their lives easier, using the right channels, but that comes down to comprehensively planning every action that you want your customers to take.

"Sales funnels still exist, but the problem with sales funnels is that they tend to make you look at things from a sales perspective, and not from a customer's point of view. How should you help your customers? How do you make their engagement with your brand flow more smoothly; and their lives easier?

"You need to consider how you plan your customer's journey, how you intend for your customers to interact with your content and how to align all your strategies to make sure that your content educates, rewards and helps.

"Is the reward that customers receive worth the information that you're asking them to hand over?"
EDWIN RAYMOND
@FLNmarketing

"Of course your content should also align with the selling of your products, or help your sales team to engage with your customers, if you're doing B2B. It should help you be more authentic and complete more sales. To do this, you should be leveraging the power of marketing automation technology such as HubSpot, Pardot or Marketing Cloud.

"To me, the 3 key questions are:

- Is your content, your funnel or your journey easy for your customers to navigate?
- Is the reward that your customers receive worth the information that you're asking them to hand over?
- How do the actions in your customer journey complement your sales team's activities?"

7) Move your customers through the *attraction, engagement* and *delight* flywheel – Kevan Lee

In the previous tip, Edwin shared that successful marketing today comes down to great planning and execution. Great planning is where Kevan Lee's tip begins. Kevan is the Director of Marketing for social media management platform, *Buffer.com*.

Kevan says, "My number one tip is to stop thinking of marketing as a funnel and to begin to think about it in terms of loops and flywheels. That's the big picture idea that we're operating with here at Buffer. The way that we're making this actionable, and the takeaway for you today is to run an exercise to come up with some answers.

> *"Stop thinking of marketing as a funnel, and begin to think about it in terms of loops and flywheels."*
> KEVAN LEE
> *@kevanlee*

"We take a lot of inspiration from the folks at HubSpot and their flywheel exercise. It goes like this: You create the initial flywheel by identifying the core ways you attract customers; the ways you engage customers and the ways you delight customers. After identifying each of those ways you attach a single success metric to each stage.

"Next, we start thinking about how we can maximize delight and how can we reduce friction. For maximizing delight, you examine all the different activities and programs that you're currently doing within marketing – the different activities that move your customers through that flywheel of attraction, engagement and delight.

"You end up with this table where you can consider whether the activities that you have listed are designed to serve your own process or your customers' needs. Ideally they're going to be designed to service your customers' needs. With each activity that you analyse, consider how you're going to use it to maximize customer delight.

"When it comes to reducing friction, we break this down using four different steps. Firstly, identify your points of friction. Think about the complaints that you hear from customers, think about goals that you've had trouble hitting in the past. Then decide which of these friction points can be automated. Of the things that can't be automated, consider what can be addressed through sharing goals with other teams in your business.

"If you can't figure out how to automate your friction points, or how to work internally to resolve them, think about how you can address them through the reorganization of your teams and departments.

"At the end of this exercise you're left with a wonderful action plan for the coming year, with multiple ways to maximize customer delight."

8) Start with a customer-centric approach to the purchase journey – Amy Bishop

Just as Kevin has his customers at the centre of the flywheel, Amy Bishop from *CultivativeMarketing.com* has a similar thought process.

Amy says: "A customer-centric approach to the purchase journey puts you in your customer's shoes. Think about the information your customers need and their decision factors before mapping your campaigns and your cross-channel touchpoints.

"To get a better pulse on funnel performance, set up micro-conversions, track the journey, and then map your audiences to the funnel. Audiences are a great tool for designing and supporting those paths, especially across multiple channels.

"Make sure that you're spending some time identifying those optimum audiences that can drive the most revenue – including first-party and third-party audiences. To do that, look in Google Analytics at your demographic and interest data, as well as the addition of some good third-party audiences.

"Even if you're not focused on building audiences right now, by doing this exercise you'll discover certain groups of people that are more likely to convert. Create custom reports in Google Analytics to identify other valuable segments worth basing audiences upon – things like page depth and time on site. Find metrics that indicate a greater propensity for that user to become a customer.

"Make sure that you're spending some time identifying those best audiences that can drive the most revenue"
AMY BISHOP
@Hoffman8

"Be sure that you have an audience report set up within Google Analytics, so that you're reviewing the performance data across all channels and campaigns.

"Once you have all of your audiences set up in Google Analytics, you can then determine which of those are proving to be the most valuable. View these audiences using custom-use segments and custom dashboards. This lets you monitor performance, but also identify opportunities to improve the performance of those audiences by discovering the content that they like best, and the referring channels that convert the best."

So would Amy generally advise that you write bespoke copy targeting specific audiences, and that you have different landing pages for different audiences?

"Absolutely. That can be really valuable. Having those audience reports set up gives you so much more opportunity to dig into what kind of content those audiences are resonating with – and then you can tailor your content to make it even more specific.

"I also highly recommend looking at site search reports – because you may discover phrases that prospects are searching for on your site that don't result in the answer that they're looking for, and they then leave your site unsatisfied. On-site search reports can be a great opportunity to create specific content for those audiences, keeping them on-site, and ultimately converting them."

9) Get to know your customer's challenges - Louise Robertson

For Louise Robertson, Global Marketing Director at *Localz.com*, it's essential that you are led by your customers' desires, rather than the other way around.

> *"Don't focus on what's easy to do and measure. Instead focus on what's more difficult – the things that are important to your customers."*
> **LOUISE ROBERTSON**
> *@localz*

Louise says: "Don't focus on what's easy to do and measure. Instead focus on what's more difficult – the things that are important to your customers.

"Know your customers' challenges, keep close to them, their market. Ask them questions and learn to listen with intent."

10) Being more user-centric can improve your digital marketing success - Alexander Royle

Sometimes it's difficult to get all the information you need from your own customers. For Alexander Royle, Head of Search for *BBC Studios* (including BBC Good Food and Top Gear), it's important that you're not afraid of doing something a little bit different.

Alexander says: "The one tip that's made the biggest impact over the past year for me is a mindset change – testing your hunches and not being afraid of failure.

"Last year, we delved into our data, looking at what our users wanted, and what our users were doing, and we tried to make all of our brands more user-centric. And it's worked incredibly well.

"Just because all of your competitors aren't doing something, it doesn't mean that you can't be the one to try it, if it's a good idea."
ALEXANDER ROYLE
@Royle88

"We tested a lot of our hunches – and we found a way to test them in a controlled environment. We gathered data, and we looked at whether or not we could roll-out successful tests for all of our digital activities.

"My main piece of advice is just don't be afraid to fail. Don't be afraid to be the first brand to try something new. Just because all of your competitors aren't doing something, it doesn't mean that you can't be the one to try it, if it's a good idea.

"For example on *BBCgoodfood.com* we altered the structure of our recipes. Anecdotally, one of the people that we work with felt that the recipes needed to be more concise, easier to follow and more readable.

"Although we were ranking first on Google, even though we were ranking first in the mobile carousel, we weren't winning the featured snippet on desktop.

"We reasoned that we should potentially move to more concise and easy-to-follow steps, changing the on-page SEO which could potentially lead to ranking drops. But we weren't afraid to test it, because we thought that if we delivered better UX to our users, this may help with our organic search rankings.

"And within a month of doing this, we'd won all of the featured snippets on the ten recipes that we tested. By not being scared, by looking at our users' data, and by becoming more user-centric, it helped our marketing efforts too."

11) Think of what your customers are likely to be searching for at each step along their journey, prior to making the final purchase decision – Laurie Wang

Someone else trying to obtain a stronger feel of their customers' mindsets is Laurie Wang from *LaurieWang.com*.

Laurie says: "I believe that the terminology 'Micro-Moments' is going to get more popular among marketers over the coming months and years. Micro-Moments is a new consumer behaviour for the digital age, and a term created by Google, helping you to deliver your marketing messaging clearly and concisely, in a way that's of interest to consumers, all within the span of seconds.

"If we don't capture the customer's imagination straight away, we can lose their attention in an instant. We see this sort of behaviour happening all the time, especially nowadays with consumers having busier and busier lifestyles.

"Nowadays, people like to make instant decisions on what to eat, which restaurants to choose, what to purchase and where to go. When I was in New York recently I used Micro-Moment style searches all the time when I was on the go. If you take the time to understand a user's mindset in each Micro-Moment, you go a long way to understanding how the customer journey is changing over time.

> *"If we don't capture the customer's imagination straight away, we can lose their attention in an instant."*
> **LAURIE WANG**
> *@iamlauriewang*

"To take advantage of Micro-Moments, make sure that your brand is active on platforms such as Google Maps, Amazon, YouTube and Google Search, and anywhere else that people search for information at a moment's notice."

12) Start by using the See, Think, Do, Care framework around your customers' journey – Patrick Cutliffe

A way to gain a better understanding of the customer journey is using Avinash Kaushik's 'See, Think, Do, Care' framework – that's what Patrick Cutliffe from *BuzzStartAcademy.com* recommends.

Patrick says: "My top tip to improve your marketing now is to start using the See, Think, Do, Care framework around your customers' journey. This involves utilizing signals of intent and Micro-Moments, as well as the See, Think, Do, Care framework.

"Start by creating a table with four column heads – See, Think, Do, Care. I want you to use a large sheet of paper or a large whiteboard in your office. And within each column, I want you to break down each of these four stages.

"The See column is your largest qualified addressable audience – basically anyone who could potentially buy your products or services. The Think column is the same audience, but only including those who are thinking about your brand, your products or services. The Do column is the same audience, but those who are extremely 'hot' and ready to buy your products or services. And then the Care column is the same audience who have purchased something from your brand more than twice.

> *"Start using the See, Think, Do, Care framework around your customers' journey."*
> **PATRICK CUTLIFFE**
> *@PatrickCutliffe*

"For example, if you represent a car brand, the See stage or column is everyone who likes to travel or move from place to place and has money. The Think stage is everyone who likes to travel, has transportation needs and are thinking about changing their vehicle, but not quite ready to buy yet. And the Do stage is all of these people who are ready to buy from you right now.

"I want you now to think about the signals of intent – the signals that your customers provide at the digital touchpoints in their journey.

"Every time that we interact with a digital device today, we provide information and signals around our intentions. As a business, you should be analysing your data sources for signals of intent and mapping your customers' signals of intent under each of the columns See, Think, Do, Care.

"For example, a customer might search for a phrase in Google. If they click on your paid ad, they'll arrive on your landing page, and they then might watch a 'how to' video. Consider the signals of intent in that scenario and how you're serving your prospects.

"In order to do so, just as Laurie shared in the previous tip, you should be thinking about Micro-Moments. We have the data insights around our customers' intent to service these Micro-Moments. It's just about using this data to deliver what our customers are looking for, just at the right time. i.e. How can you best serve your customers on their journey with relevant timely content using the data that you already have?

"If your customer wants to learn something, make sure you provide it where they are digitally at that moment in time, in a manner that's convenient for them. If your customer wants to discover something, make sure you appear in the search results. If they want to watch something, make sure that you've created video content. If they want to buy something, make them an offer.

"Create your See, Think, Do, Care framework and put it on your wall. Start mapping-out your customers' journey. And use user-signals and Micro-Moments as part of the process."

13) Experiment with your landing pages – start by writing good sales copy – Isaac Rudansky

Although Isaac Rudansky from *AdventurePPC.com* is a top technical marketer, he's still an advocate for great copywriting.

Isaac says: "I think the most important thing for marketers to do is to experiment with their landing pages. That's something that a lot of marketers aren't doing. It's unbelievable how many clients we have that are testing their ads, but when it comes to their landing pages – where the main customer experience happens – they're doing very little testing.

"There's a couple of reasons behind this. Firstly, it's difficult. It's hard for marketers to get buy-in from upper management in a company. Because typically, what a landing page says and what a landing page looks like is really what the boss or the person at the top of the chain wants it to say or look like.

"But if you use the three stages of conversion-rate optimization experiments, you could see enormous improvements:

i) Diagnosing
ii) Implementing tests
iii) Analysing results

"If you could increase your conversion rate by just a few percentage points, you'll then have additional money to put into traffic acquisition, which is what most companies are spending most of their time doing.

"Try using tools like Usability Hub (*https://usabilityhub.com/*) to run preference tests by showing 50 visitors home page version one, and 50 visitors version two. Give them five seconds each to take a look at your page. You then ask everyone who's viewed the web page, 'What does this company do?' This is what's called the five-second preference test. It's a very famous test in usability.

"To run this sort of experiment, show a screenshot of your landing page to 50 people. Then alter the screenshot to use a different headline and a different sub-headline for another set of 50 people. Ask both lots of people the same questions:

- 'What does this company do?'
- 'What value do they provide their customers?'

"I've done these sorts of tests over and over again and I've found that a lot of companies like to have really catchy headlines that don't really mean anything by themselves. The clarity of the products or services tend to get articulated in the sub-headlines.

"I've experimented just switching the sub-headline with the headline and running a preference test. Nine times out of 10, we'll have significantly better responses from anonymous users that understand the version with the original sub-heading as the heading compared with the original version!

> *"The thing that really makes an impact when it comes to conversion rate – if you want to increase conversion rate – is testing copy."*
> **ISAAC RUDANSKY**
> *@isaacrudansky*

"When you put the sub-headline where the headline is, they have a much better understanding of what the company actually does, which is what your landing page and website needs to do really quickly if you want to have a chance of converting your visitors or getting your visitors interested in your products or services.

"This is all part of the diagnosing stage, doing some preference tests, determining where the copy on your landing pages isn't so clear and testing the performance of your headlines. To do this you could use a tool like Google Optimize. You could also use Visual Website Optimizer or Optimizely. Whatever tool you use, just start running some

A/B tests. Run 50% of your traffic to see headline A and 50% of your traffic see headline B.

"The last thing to remember is not to spend too much time testing meaningless elements. People love to test button colours. They love to test one image versus another image. They love to test font and typography. These things are really easy to test because it's aesthetics which is something that comes naturally to many marketers, but these tests don't tend to change nearly as much when it comes to conversion rate. The thing that really makes an impact if you want to increase conversion rate is testing copy.

"Testing copy is difficult because it's not easy to write good copy. You have to understand your principles of salesmanship, which is a very, very important thing to know as a marketer. Two books that I'd recommend are 'Persuasion' by Robert Cialdini and 'Scientific Advertising' by Claude Hopkins. These are two fantastic books if you want to get better at testing your landing pages, testing your copy and writing better, more persuasive copy."

14) Sales and marketing is still an emotional business – Stewart Rogers

Someone else who is completely up-to-speed with how technology advancements are impacting marketing is Analyst-at-large for *VentureBeat* and Managing Editor at *Grit Daily*, Stewart Rogers from *StewartRogers.me*. However, Stewart advocates a more holistic understanding of your consumers.

Stewart says: "Artificial intelligence has started to take over marketing technology since 2017. That's fine. It's doing all sorts of cool stuff for us. It's helping us to see the future with predictive analytics. It's helping us to automate all of our communications. It's helping us to do all of these amazing things. But there's something that is absolutely actionable that everybody needs to remember to do… and that something isn't just letting the technology take over (that's a really bad idea).

"Sales and marketing is still an emotional business. If you do not elicit an emotional response from the consumer, from the user, from the person that wants to give you their business, you are not going to get that money! If you can't make them *feel* something, they're not going to give you any of their hard-earned cash.

"Regardless of artificial intelligence, marketing technology and anything else that is out there, there is a tool that can help you to sell or market your products or services – and that tool is emotion!

> *"Sales and marketing is still an emotional business. If you do not elicit an emotional response from the consumer…you are not going to get that money!"*
> **STEWART ROGERS**
> *@TheRealSJR*

"I was onstage at Slush in Helsinki recently, and we were talking about companies that do a really good job at eliciting emotion. One of the companies that came up in the discussion was BrewDog. There's millions of breweries around the world, and let's be honest, they all produce amazing products. It's beer! You can't go wrong!

"However, BrewDog have managed to stand out from the rest of the breweries because every single press release they distribute has 45 swear words in it! They have brands like Punk IPA. They have stood out from the crowd, and they've created something that elicits an emotional response; and that's why they have become so incredibly popular.

"Do that. Let the technology work for you, but make sure that you're still creating an emotional reaction in your customers, otherwise you're screwed! Simple as that!"

Chapter 1: Getting Started & Best Practice – summary

i) Take the best content that you published last year and build a strategy that leverages it for new prospects

ii) Never lose sight of the aim to achieve digital performance perfection, teaching everyone in your business about the impact that their role has on your companies' overall digital success

iii) Get your priorities right and start spending more time on marketing activities that are more likely to have a massive upside

iv) Ensure that internal marketing data is shared between departments, and that digital marketing efforts are as aligned as much as possible

v) Focus on helping your customers achieve their objectives

vi) Ensure that your customer journey is easy to navigate and that it compliments your sales team's activities

vii) Create a 'marketing flywheel', identifying the core ways you attract customers, engage customers and delight customers.

viii) Build audiences in Google Analytics that are more likely to convert by finding the commonalities which make those audiences more likely to engage with your brand

ix) Know your customers' challenges and keep close to them – ask them questions and learn to listen with intent

x)   Don't be afraid to test new things that are likely to have a positive impact on user behaviour – even though they go against conventional marketing wisdom

xi)   Take the time to understand a user's train of thought in each 'micro-moment' to go a long way to understanding how the customer journey is changing

xii)   Gain a better understanding of your customer's journey using Avinash Kaushik's 'See, Think, Do, Care' framework

xiii)   Get great at writing copy to improve your conversion rates and put the increased profits back into traffic acquisition

xiv)   Don't let technology control you – create something that elicits an emotional response from your target audience

Before you move on to the second chapter, if you haven't done so already, go to *DavidBain.com/MarketingNow* and sign-up to watch our free implementation workshops where we delve into specific examples of how different types of businesses can action the advice shared in Marketing Now.

2

BRAND, VIDEO & AUTHENTICITY

I n Chapter 2 of Marketing Now it's time to define you and your brand to your target audience – and to encourage that audience to like, trust and believe in what you do.

15) Focus on brand - Ross Tavendale

Ross Tavendale, Managing Director of *TypeAMedia.net* loves what he calls 'messing about' with SEOs when they're chatting about the latest techniques in their specialist field.

Ross explains: "When SEOs ask me what the key things are that they should be focusing on over the coming year, I like to say that my number one ranking factor, the most important thing for next year is… brand. And I just watch their faces go, 'did that guy just say brand is the most important thing'?

"So what does brand bring me as an organic search agency owner? We're a tiny little boutique agency based out of London, but for some reason, our deal flow is amazing, despite not really ranking for a ton of stuff. That's because the stuff we do rank for is incredibly commercial.

"When it comes to converting prospects, or putting them through link magnets, it's so easy for us – because we have this little microbrand 'thing' going on.

"We do a lot of link building, and we build links in some of the biggest publications in the world, from the BBC to the Wall Street Journal. What we find is that if we're working for start-ups and they've got no brand equity, or they're not an obvious entity with enough online trust, there's a dampening effect on the link value that we build. Thus, the importance of brand.

"If you're doing video – I'll have to thank David for being so instrumental in helping me with this – you need to make sure that your visuals and your audio is great. That's all part of how people perceive your brand too.

> *"Take a very small amount of the budget you've got and put it into brand."*
> **ROSS TAVENDALE**
> *@rtavs*

"The reason why video, for me, is such a big play when it comes to brand is because we use something called a COPE strategy. Create Once, Publish Everywhere.

"If you think about what a video is, it's moving pictures and audio, so you can strip out the pictures and turn them into nice quote cards. You can also publish the audio as a podcast.

"That's what we like to do for our clients, taking a very small amount of the budget and putting it into authority-building brand work, just squeezing it, making it work as hard as possible."

16) Watch what your customers do, and then engage with them personally - Brigitta Jordaan

For Brigitta Jordaan, a freelance brand and marketing consultant, authenticity and personalization will be key elements in her marketing success over the coming year.

Brigitta says: "More and more brands are adopting digital automation strategies and tactics. These tactics help brands to become more agile. However, automation can be a barrier to creating authentic and personal consumer relationships.

> *"Moments of personal interaction have become one of the leading factors influencing brand consideration"*
> **BRIGITTA JORDAAN**
> *@brigs_01*

"It's now even more important in this age of digital transformation to focus on building meaningful and authentic personal and interactive engagement with consumers. Moments of personal interaction have become one of the leading factors influencing brand consideration, and ultimately brand support.

"While personalization is not something new, behaviour-based personalization and engagement will be a far more effective approach as time goes by."

In other words, watch what your customers do, and engage with them personally to cement the deal.

17) Take an authenticity inventory - Lida Citroën

Lida Citroën, Founder of *LIDA360.com* believes that personal interaction can be, and should be planned. Lida says: "I think the word that we keep coming back to, which is sometimes is a little overused, is authenticity. Brands that are authentic, companies that are authentic, can hold themselves accountable. They can admit their mistakes. They can rise to the occasion when it's called for.

"As marketers, we target, market and create online personas for our products, celebrities, endorsers, executives etc. But we often forget when we're targeting one channel – maybe it's Instagram or something else – that information can get shared by consumers on other channels. This means that we have to make sure that whatever we share is always authentic.

"I came out of corporate marketing, where everything was about packaging and presentation, making sure it was perfect. But now, marketing is about authenticity – as overused a word as it might be.

> *"The consumer is smart enough to know if and when there's a fracture in your story"*
> **LIDA CITROËN**
> *@LIDA360*

"Take a digital swath or inventory of your online presence, as an individual or as a company and make sure that all of those touchpoints are consistent. They don't have to be perfect, but they need to tell the same story. Because the consumer is smart enough to know if and when there's a fracture in your story – then the whole deck of cards can fall down.

"Don't say that you believe in something or you value something if you really don't. Consumers are smart enough to know that we can all value and believe in different things – but promises are really important online.

"Take that digital inventory – do an assessment. Remove what isn't working and clean it up going forward."

"An example of a fracture in authenticity could be when somebody else writes the CEO's Twitter or LinkedIn messages – we want to hear from the CEO! We want to hear from that individual specifically. There are high-profile cases where the CEO has tried to tweet or blog under a pseudonym. That generally doesn't work out well. As consumers we've become smarter to recognise who's really doing the talking.

"One of the specialties that I focus on is reputation repair and I make sure that my clients don't make those sorts of mistakes, because it's a lot more expensive to unwind it, than it is to just be authentic out of the gate!"

18) Any business that has a physical location needs to pay more attention to *Google My Business* and *Google Posts* – Greg Gifford

Another essential part of brand trust – certainly if you're a business with a physical location – is your ability to portray where you are, what you do and why people should do business with you in Google's local search listings.

Greg Gifford from *Wikimotive.com* says: "Anyone that has a business with a physical location, or serves customers in a particular geographic area really needs to pay more attention to *Google My Business*.

"Google My Business is the new homepage of your website if you're a local business. All the things that the customer used to go to your website for – such as directions, a little bit more about you as a brand, testimonials, your phone number, pictures of your business – this all now happens on Google's Knowledge Panel.

"A lot of business owners aren't paying attention to this. Google is now often the first impression that customers get of your brand, like your homepage used to be. You need to complete all the information about your business that you can in Google My Business. Select the right categories and upload awesome photos and videos.

"Pay attention to Google Q&A, which now shows on desktop, and has done for the last year – and still, hardly anyone knows it's there. Load in your own questions. Answer your own questions. Pay attention to the answers that appear and upvote your own answers to show them as the definitive answers.

"You also need to be using Google Posts (*posts.withgoogle.com*) to share promotional information that you want to publish. There's a lot of different things within Google My Business that's incredibly important to local business success.

> *"Google My Business is the new homepage of your website if you're a local business."*
> **GREG GIFFORD**
> *@GregGifford*

"With Google Posts for example, it's really important to choose the right images. A lot of marketers aren't paying attention to how Google crops their images. They're actually cropped slightly differently between desktop and mobile – so if you're going to have text on your images, pay attention to how that's displayed.

"There are different types of Posts that you can publish. Pay attention to what text is going to be displayed in the thumbnail view of your image, because you only get one line of characters, so it's really tough to display anything compelling there.

"We've received insane levels of success for a lot of our clients by using Posts, and using them correctly. Now you can upload videos too, so you've got a video thumbnail. When you click on it, it auto-plays, so experiment with that too.

"This is really important, especially now that Google allows consumers to follow your business. For instance, if a customer has an Android phone, whenever they open Google Maps it's going to serve up Posts from the businesses that they follow. This is going to be huge over the coming few years."

19) Make the most of local search and Google My Business specifically - Syed Ali

Greg's tips are reflected by Syed Ali, Head of Search at *iThinkMedia.co.uk*. Syed says: "If I could give one piece of advice when it comes to marketing success at the moment it would be to make the most of local search – and Google My Business specifically.

> *"Make sure you are using the functionality provided within Google My Business to the max!"*
> **SYED ALI**
> *@iThinkMediaUK*

"Google is aggressively developing and promoting this product – which aligns with a surge in local searches from their users. Make sure that you are using the functionality provided within Google My Business to the max! It's a great way to let Google know that you are a local entity, which means that they can understand you as a brand or business.

"This doesn't just apply to small local single-store businesses. It applies equally to bigger businesses with 100+ branches or stores just as much as individual restaurants and beauty salons. If your business has a physical address, take advantage of this opportunity now!"

20) Video, video, video - Rebekah Radice

For Rebekah Radice from *RebekahRadice.com*, the way to ramp-up your presence in the modern digital world is to do more with video. Rebekah says: "My tip has been the same for the past several years, which is live video. Live video has really dominated the social and content space recently – and with good reason.

"Just looking at the soaring popularity that live video has brought over the last few years, you cannot afford:

a) not be invested in video
b) think YouTube only.

"Today there's Facebook Live, Instagram, LinkedIn and more – there are so many different options where we can connect with our audience. You also have to be thinking about how you can strategically repurpose content that you've created as a live video.

> *"For marketing now we shouldn't be hiding behind our computers"*
> **REBEKAH RADICE**
> *@RebekahRadice*

"Whether it's pre-created video or live-streamed video, there's a variety of ways that you can connect with your customers in a personalised manner, and I see that as our big opportunity at the moment – not only to get in front of, but to stay in front of your audience and participate in conversations.

"For marketing now we shouldn't be hiding behind our computers, nor hiding behind our content, but getting actively involved, and really listening to what our audience is interested in.

"I have put together a P-R-E-P method to help with this – it's a framework that simplifies how to be planning, researching, executing and profiting from your video content. Check it out over at *RebekahRadice.com/prep-performance.*"

21) Use live video to demonstrate authenticity - Ian Anderson Gray

Another big proponent of live video and the authenticity that this can bring is Ian Anderson Gray from *iag.me.* Ian says: "I think a lot of people are talking about this word, authenticity. But we have to rethink what it really means.

"You've got to be strategic in the live video that you do, and you should be injecting some of your own humanity into your live video. Live video is a great way for us to bring ourselves in front of the audience. It allows you to connect with your audience, and allows them to have access to us.

"It's those funny, unscripted moments, when something doesn't come out quite so well that makes live video so fun and engaging."
IAN ANDERSON GRAY
@iagdotme

"You need to be focusing on exploring what authenticity means - to perhaps be more vulnerable when you're on live video. Embrace the imperfections. Production quality doesn't always have to be so slick. It's those funny, unscripted moments, when something doesn't come out quite so well that makes live video so fun and engaging.

"The other thing is to be smarter with live video. I don't think that it's a good idea to do live video just for the sake of doing it. There needs to be a strategy behind it. One of the great things about live video is that it can be a great way to create high quality content, quickly.

"I recently wrote a blog post which was 10,000 words long, and it took me two-and-a-half weeks of solid work. It was a huge amount of effort and it's going to be amazing for me, in terms of evergreen content. When you create live video, you can create half-an-hour of live video, and then from that, repurpose it intelligently across multiple platforms. You can edit your recorded video for YouTube and you can turn it into a podcast. You can turn it into a blog post. Extract all the value from your live video in different forms.

"Live video is a great way to start creating content quickly, over multiple platforms. That's what I'm going to be focusing on it over the coming year and I definitely think that you should be exploring it too."

22) Start creating video content and use Facebook to promote it - Gavin Bell

Someone else who's keen on video and how to blend social advertising, understanding consumer behaviour and the power of video together is Gavin Bell from *MrGavinBell.com*. Gavin says: "I like to focus on consumer behaviour, on human beings. This includes the things we've done as human beings for hundreds of years and what we'll continue to do in the future.

"Although I focus on Facebook Ads with my agency, it's important to think about how we use consumer behaviour and Facebook Ads together.

"There are still marketers in businesses who aren't creating content for their customers, content that their customers are searching for, questions that their customers are asking, problems that their customers are needing solved. A lot of marketers aren't creating that type of content, and they're certainly not creating it in video form.

"I speak on quite a few stages a year and I ask the audience the same question every single time - 'Who's thought about creating video content?' Most of the hands in the room go up. Then I ask: 'Who's actually doing it?' Three or four hands will stay up. Most people aren't creating video. My number one tip is to get people to start creating video content – even if they don't know what to create right now. Just start and get into the habit of creating it. That will take you on a journey of finding things that work for you and finding things that don't work for you.

> *"Create video content and use Facebook Ads to promote your video content, driving people further into your funnel."*
> **GAVIN BELL**
> *@MrGavinBell*

"Further to that, start using Facebook Ads to promote the video content that you create for consumers who are going to be interested in that specific piece of content. This is really effective because you start to build an audience of people that have consumed your videos and may be interested in being a customer of yours in the future.

"What we can then do on Facebook is create retargeting ads to the people who have consumed our video content. This takes me back to the first point I made about consumer behaviour. We only buy things from people that we know, like and trust. So provide value first – i.e. video content. And retarget those people with follow-up ads. By the time they see that follow-up ad, dropped into a lead magnet, they already know who we are – and hopefully, they already like and trust us, so they're much more likely to take the action to become a lead, and then a customer. Create video content and use Facebook Ads to promote your video content, driving people further into your funnel."

23) You'll miss out if you're not doing video – Jim Banks

A recent convert to video content is Jim Banks, CEO of *SpadesMedia.com*. Jim believes that we're currently at what he calls an 'inflexion point' in digital marketing. Jim says: "You need to invest in video, because thanks to smartphones, everyone's now a content producer.

"Much of the evolution that's assisted the rapid growth of video has actually been on the data side of things. T-Mobile have implemented a 5G back-bone in 1000 cities around the world. To give you an idea of what this means for internet connection speed, 5G allows a 25 gig UHD video could be downloaded in just 10 seconds!

> *"If you haven't got video as the front-and-centre, integral part of your content strategy, you're going to miss out."*
> **JIM BANKS**
> *@jimbanks*

"We're finding that the ads that we run on Facebook and Instagram perform so much better with video compared with static images. If you haven't incorporated video into your marketing strategy yet, now's the time to do it.

"Cisco stats say that 82% of all internet traffic will be video by 2020, so if you haven't got video as the front-and-centre, integral part of your content strategy, you're going to miss out."

24) Make one-minute videos, and make them real and imperfect - Dennis Yu

However, don't get caught up trying to make your videos too perfect. According to Dennis Yu, Chief Technology Officer at *BlitzMetrics.com*, quick, 'real' videos can perform a lot better than videos that you take a long time to pre-plan. To prove his point, Dennis joined me on the call live from a Mexican diner! Dennis says: "When you make 1-minute videos that lack in professional production quality, people are more likely to believe you, and want to engage with you because it's real and imperfect.

"Yesterday we had dinner at Abuelo's restaurant and prior to that we had a professional video shoot with six live cameras. We were at the Digital Marketer headquarters, with people who have a ton of expertise, talking about these same sorts of things, our top marketing tips – and let me tell you what, the content sucked!

"The number one guy in landing page and conversion optimization will probably have an ugly page, because ugly makes the money!"
DENNIS YU
@dennisyu

"The content was plastic! It felt like a staged interview. We're all wearing these different mics, and the vibe just wasn't there. All the speakers went out afterwards to have drinks, and we had an amazing discussion over drinks – and we said, 'You know what? *That* should have been the thing that we taped.' Think about the best things that you learn, the best discussions that you have – they're real life, not staged.

"I have professional video equipment in my backpack and I didn't pull it out to record this. I am literally streaming here on a MacBook Pro from a diner. Me and my friend are hanging out and having drinks – and I'm eating some catfish right now! Even though that has nothing to do with the latest tips on Facebook, that's how the viewer knows it's legit. People want to see and hear reality.

"Make one-minute, vertical videos, and post them on Facebook and LinkedIn, and watch what happens. The last video I posted on LinkedIn went to 25,000 impressions, because I'm posting 'real' vertical videos that are only a minute or two long. And almost nobody's doing it! It's a wide open opportunity right now!"

So what about producing videos for ads on Facebook? Does Dennis use this type of 'real' video for ads as well?

"Absolutely. And then we boost it, and we find it out-performs the $50,000 professional video."

And is that in terms of the view time or conversation rates?

"In terms of driving people into the store, in terms of driving sales, driving phone calls, driving leads, in terms of making money. Do you want to make money? Usually the ugliest thing to talk about, right? The number one guy in landing page and conversion optimization will probably have an ugly page, because ugly makes the money! Do you want to be pretty or do you want to make money?!"

25) Video should start off as a sales initiative that feeds marketing, not the other way around - Marcus Sheridan

Someone else who's developed a video strategy that measurably impacts the bottom line is Marcus Sheridan from *MarcusSheridan.com*.

Marcus says: "A couple of years ago my agency wondered if it was really possible for companies to develop an in-house video culture. We went on a mission to make it happen. During this time we helped to create a whole plethora of video types, specifically focused on sales and generating significant business.

"It's interesting, most people see video as a marketing initiative. Video should start off as a sales initiative that feeds marketing, not the other way around.

"The one video that we've developed which has had the greatest impact on sales is what we call the 80% video. If you create this type of video, it's going to have a big-time impact. This strategy is for anybody on your sales team, or for any of your employees that integrate with your sales process.

"Most people see video as a marketing initiative. Video should start off as a sales initiative that feeds marketing, not the other way around."
MARCUS SHERIDAN
@TheSalesLion

"First, take the major products or services that you sell – if you sell a lot of them, just choose the top 20% that generate 80% of your revenue, and research the major questions that you get asked every time a prospect enquires about this particular product or service.

"There's a good chance that if you talk to anybody that's on a sales team, they're going to say that they typically get the same questions every time they speak to a customer.

"Ideally, per product or per service, you want to choose the top seven questions that prospects tend to ask you. Seven is what we've seen to be the best number. You should create one video that addresses all seven of those common questions as honestly and transparently as possible. Once you've created that video, the next thing that you should do is to immediately integrate it into your sales process.

"Let's say that you're going to have a sales call with a prospect in a few days' time. Say before the call: 'I want you to watch this because I know you will have a set of questions, worries, and concerns right now. We've created this video that addresses all those major concerns that people just like you have – and if you watch this, our time together is going to be dramatically more effective, and you won't be making any mistakes.

"If you produce such a video, you should consider integrating it into your automated responses too. There are different ways to utilise this strategy, but it's one of the most powerful marketing techniques that we've seen and it's so uncanny how few companies do this! Because if you do talk to anyone that works in sales, they'll say, 'I keep getting the same old questions over and over again'.

"The whole idea is that we eliminate 80% of the questions that are redundant before we talk to the prospect. That way, when we talk with them, we're spending less time teaching and more time selling. That's the 80% video."

Who should be in front of the camera? The sales person or someone else from the business?

"We've done so much work looking into this! I didn't realise that on-camera performance training was going to be such a big deal! Most people say 'we're not good on camera', or 'I'm not good on camera', but if you go to that same person, whether it's a typical subject matter expert or a sales person and you say 'Are you good with people?' They're going to say yes. This is because we don't see the camera as people, or as the customer.

"The moment that we see the camera as the customer is the moment we start to change, and we become dramatically more comfortable. The person that should produce this type of video ideally should be the one that is going to be meeting with the prospect, that's going to have that personal relationship. If not that person, at least somebody that represents your brand well and can articulate the tone, the voice and the style that you're trying to get across. The more you can individualise this, the better."

How often should this kind of video be updated? Is once a year enough?

"Yes, in most cases, once a year is enough – unless you're in an incredibly fluid industry where things are constantly changing. I have some videos that are just as relevant from a sales perspective as when I created them three years ago. We've got other videos that we have to update every six months.

"We've all got to develop this culture that thinks of what we do as a media company – whether we like it or not. This is where we're all headed as a society and as businesses. Once we embrace that, and really tap into this whole power of visual marketing and the visual sale, it gets really magical."

Chapter 2: Brand, Video and Authenticity – summary

   i)   Building your brand will help the rest of your marketing activities – put a small amount of your marketing budget aside to just focus on brand

   ii)   Personal interaction is key to influencing brand consideration – interact with your prospects on a one-to-one basis to enhance your brand's perception

   iii)   Ensure that your business and personal brands are congruent, sharing the same ethos everywhere. Conduct an authenticity inventory

iv) If your business has a physical location, optimize your Google My Business listing and leverage the power of Google Posts

v) A Google My Business listing also gives Google greater confidence about your business, as well as how and where it should be featuring your business in its listings

vi) Broadcasting live video is an incredible marketing opportunity right now – it's dominating many aspects of social media, so take advantage of it now

vii) Live video also helps you demonstrate authenticity – don't be afraid of getting it wrong – i.e. it's those funny, unscripted moments, when something doesn't come out quite so well that makes live video so fun and engaging

viii) Create engaging videos for Facebook that don't try to directly sell what you do – then build retargeting campaigns for those who watch your videos

ix) You need to invest in video, because thanks to smartphones, everyone's now a content producer

x) Don't spend a lot of time having professionally produced videos made for Facebook – when you make 1-minute videos that lack in professional production quality, people are more likely to believe you and engage with you because it's real and imperfect

xi) Pick the 7 most common questions asked about your product and have your sales person answer those questions in a video; use that video as part of your pre-sales process and marketing funnel

3

TECH & AUTOMATION

A customer's digital experience of your brand isn't limited to product, price and positioning. If you're not delivering a fast, efficient experience, you'll be dampening down the impact of the rest of your marketing efforts.

26) Double-down on your tech stack - Fabrizio Ballarini

Fabrizio Ballarini, Head of Organic Growth and SEO at *TransferWise.com* advises you to double-down on your own tech stack over the coming year. Fabrizio says: "There are a lot of technologies that you could be focusing on such as voice search, APIs, JavaScript, AMP, PWAs and many other things that help you to automate what was manually done in the past.

"The more I speak to companies, the more I realise that they increasingly have challenges in their marketing teams to implement their strategies, just because they are stuck on making the engineering resources available.

"What that ultimately leads to is that they're not developing product as much as they could – and not improving their customer experiences on the web as much as they could.

"I would focus on two areas when you're doubling-down on tech. One is on talent. First, hire an engineer – no matter what your team is doing. I would suggest that you make this hire anyway, no matter how much you're involved with technical stuff, so that you can first-of-all unlock dev resources in the team. In doing so, you make it so much more likely that your marketing strategy can actually be implemented.

> *"If you're really serious about your product's content, you should be equally serious about the tech that you own"*
> **FABRIZIO BALLARINI**
> *@Pechnet*

"The second part is to double-down on your own technology, especially if you're a web business. If you're really serious about your product's content, you should be equally serious about the tech that you own – and the amount of time and resources that you invest in your own tech. What I mean by that is anything from the marketing tools that you use for one specific task, to platforms you use throughout your business.

"This is all doubly important if you're looking to scale in the long term. Often companies embrace solutions that are easy and fast, because you can plug them in off-the-shelf. But the more scale you want, the more challenging it is to achieve that. It takes time and resources, but if you want to scale in the future, it's important to invest in your technology now."

27) Embrace the power of edge workers and go serverless - Chris Green

Someone else who's been analysing new ways to improve the experience of his clients and customers through better use of technology is Chris Green, Head of Search at *StrategiQ.co*. Chris says: "Marketing needs to embrace the power of edge workers, and the power that they can bring.

"For those of you who aren't really aware, edge workers are ways of controlling applications, utilising infrastructure on someone else's network. The ones we use are on Cloudflare's network. Using edge workers has tons of advantages – it helps you scale applications, you don't have to worry about the limits of your infrastructure anymore, it makes the aspect of tech someone else's problem!

"If you're having issues implementing coding for your marketing team right now, edge workers might just be what you're looking for!"
CHRIS GREEN
@chrisgreen87

"There was a survey that Will Critchlow from *Distilled.net* conducted a couple of years ago – he found that 60 percent of marketers in large organisations didn't expect their coding requests to have been implemented within six months! This was largely because of impenetrable tech infrastructures or CMS's that couldn't do what they wanted to do. What we're developing on edge workers will allow marketers to push these changes in-between the server and the client in ways that bypasses development queues.

"It will also allow marketers to perform SEO and A/B split-testing, without ridiculous associated infrastructure costs.

With edge workers you can conduct user-level split-testing for conversion rates and collect log file information. You can inject Schema and other data, and do other things your CMS can't do, without having huge dev queues.

"Start thinking about the possibilities of edge workers. If you're having issues implementing coding for your marketing team right now, edge workers might just be what you're looking for!"

28) Rationalise your martech stack - Scott Brinker

For Scott Brinker, Editor of *ChiefMartec.com*, your focus shouldn't be on adding to your tech stack. He has a different angle on technology use. Scott says: "I advise you to take the time to rationalise your martech stack. The first step of that is getting a good inventory of all the different tools that you're using in marketing and sales.

> *"Take the time to rationalise your martech stack."*
> **SCOTT BRINKER**
> *@chiefmartec*

"Almost every company I've seen go through this, no matter how large or small, when they actually do the search to discover who in their organisation are using different tools, the list is much longer than anyone could ever imagine. I've seen companies with 20 people do the list and say – 'oh my goodness, we have 80 tools!'

"Secondly, map out your tools on a whiteboard or on a spreadsheet and establish how the various technologies connect together. Ask 'Are we sharing data?' and 'Where's the workflow between these tools?'

"This is a great opportunity to get rid of tools that you're not using, and to make sure that you're using the tools that you choose to keep as effectively as possible.

"The last thing I would do is to take a long, hard look at the utilisation of each tool. If you have a tool that no-one's using, that's easy, get rid of it. But if you have a tool, that someone's been using the same way for a year, it's worthwhile raising the question of whether or not you should be getting more value from it."

Great advice and a valuable exercise that Scott recommends repeating once every six months.

29) Stay on top of how you can use martech - Michael Fleischner

Someone else who recommends zeroing-in on marketing technology and what it is going to be doing for you over the coming period is Michael Fleischner, Co-Founder at *BigFinSolutions.com*.

Michael says: "We're really seeing a sea change with regards to the different types of technologies that are being used to enhance marketing campaigns.

"There are two ways to take a look at this:

i) What new technologies can you integrate into your marketing technology stack?
ii) How can those technologies help you perform better and get more from the dollars that you are spending?

"Even if you're using a small software-as-a-service tool like Moz or a programmatic tool for pay-per-click marketing, take the time to ensure that you're getting the most you possibly can for your business from the tool.

"There are so many free educational resources today, whether you just visit YouTube or within the different marketing technology platforms themselves, use the free information out there to help you leverage the fullest potential of all the tools that you select.

"It behoves all of us to stay on top of everything that's happening with martech"
MICHAEL FLEISCHNER
@mfleischner

"In general, the evolution of marketing technology is something to watch, and stay on top of. We're seeing it evolve on a global scale. There are over 7,000 martech providers today. Adobe recently announced their acquisition of Marketo, in addition to Adobe Experience Cloud, which is a larger platform for enterprise-level organisations.

"It behoves all of us to stay on top of everything that's happening with martech, artificial intelligence, machine learning and natural language programming. The future is here!"

30) Use systems, automation and centralisation to make your marketing operations more efficient - Yann Ilunga

On a related note, Yann Ilunga from *YannIlunga.com* emphasises the need to optimize your own systems at the same time as optimizing your use of 3rd party marketing technology.

Yann begins: "I have three keywords that I suggest you stay on top of. The first keyword is **systems**, the second is **automation**, and the third is **centralization**.

i) Systems

"What I mean by systems are procedures that help with your creative workflows. Things like researching and gathering content ideas, or how your content creation process works. Consider the steps that you and your team carry out on a regular basis to get each task done, and organise them in a project management tool like ClickUp, Trello, Asana or Plutio.

> *"Try to save some of your valuable time and merge all of your data into all-in-one dashboards such as CYFE.com."*
> **YANN ILUNGA**
> *@TheYannilunga*

"An example of systems applied to the podcasting field could be if you host an interview-based show, to stop emailing back and forth with your guests and create or streamline the steps. Determine what you want to get from a guest – their name, their website, their headshot, etc. All these things you should be able to get in one step if you have the right system set up. It will also be a lot easier to access the information afterwards.

ii) Automation

"Automation should be pretty straightforward in this context as it is intended to automate the system you've already designed, as discussed above. You shouldn't obsess with automation, but it can really help you out.

"Let's go back to podcasting for an example. Instead of having a form that your guest fills out, and having your assistant copy and paste that into a Word doc, and then you using that as your notes while you interview your guest, try using use a tool like Trello and connecting it to your scheduling tool.

"This way, as soon as the guest gives you their name, website, and all the other data that you ask for, all the data is automatically organised in a Trello card for you. It's ready for you as soon as you want to prepare to host the interview.

"Other tools that I would recommend you check out in relation to automation are things like Zapier and IFTTT. And if you use Trello, check out Butler for Trello – it's a great tool to automate steps in Trello. *[Editor's note: Butler for Trello has recently been acquired by Trello.]*

iii) Centralization

"Whenever possible, try to avoid jumping from tool to tool. I.e. stop checking your website analytics, social media metrics and paid advertising campaign stats all in separate places. Save some of your valuable time and merge all of these stats into all-in-one dashboards such as *CYFE.com*. Centralize that data.

"Remember those three words for the coming period – systems, automation, and centralization."

31) Make better use of your time - Arianne Donoghue

Arianne Donoghue from *Edit.co.uk* also believes that automation has a key part to play in marketing now – but she says that many marketers don't know where to start.

Arianne says: "We are entering a phase in marketing where we've got ever more platforms to manage, and things are becoming so much more complicated. We've got to do more with less time and more with less money. I would really encourage you to have a look at how automation can save you time in the coming months.

"There are three key areas in particular - reporting, bidding, and analysis, where tools like Google Data Studio and scripts and platforms like Adalysis and OPTMYZR can help free-up time that you can spend on more important work.

"There can be a time or cost investment in some of these platforms, but given that your time also has value, I'd encourage you to look into how much time you could save by automating more in these areas.

"Try Toggl.com, and use that to identify where
the majority of your time goes"
ARIANNE DONOGHUE
@ArianneDonoghue

"If you don't know where to begin, try platforms like *Toggl.com* or use any time sheet data that they may have on hand. Use that to identify where the majority of your time goes, or the things that you do most repetitively. That's the best place to begin with saving your time, freeing yourself up to focus on areas that can add a lot more value."

32) Automate tedious and boring work that is currently done by humans - Steven van Vessum

For Steven van Vessum, VP of Community at *ContentKing*, automation is also an opportunity to automate tedious and boring work.

Steven says: "There are a lot of activities that are manually done, but can largely be automated. When someone's off sick or goes on holiday, or gets pulled into a meeting, are you still able to get the important tasks done?

"I'm talking about automation such as setting up alerts in Google Analytics. For instance, when your revenue drops by more than 5%, you should be getting an alert. You could do the same thing for conversions, traffic drops, and implement that across multiple channels. This can save you a lot of time instead of trying to do it all manually.

"Something else you should be automatically monitoring is brand mentions. You can use Google Alerts for this but it doesn't really work that well in my experience. There's an alternative called *Mention.com*. They do something similar. An added benefit is that you can also use these brand monitoring tools for link building as well – by asking for unlinked brand citations that you discover to be linked.

"The time that you free up with the automation, you can spend that on the things that computers cannot do yet, such as writing quality content"
STEVEN VAN VESSUM
@Stevenvvessum

"*Ahrefs* is another tool you can use to automate some of your marketing tasks. Use it to monitor links that are gained or lost. This is really useful stuff for when you're doing outreach. And of course, you can also use our very own ContentKing for managing and monitoring on-page SEO issues, and big changes on your site.

"All of this automated monitoring is much more efficient than hitting F5 all the time you're on the website that you're monitoring. Make sure that you automate everything that's possible to automate.

"This doesn't mean that you need to completely rely on automation. You still need to get a feel for what's happening on your sites. You still need to perform some manual checks too.

But for the most part, a lot of the manual tasks that marketers do can be automated.

"As Arianne highlighted in the previous tip, you can also spend the time that you free up through increased automation on the things that computers cannot do yet – such as writing quality content and generally being more creative."

Chapter 3: Tech & Automation – summary

    i)   Invest in your engineering team to make it much more likely that your marketing strategy can be implemented

    ii)   If you're having issues implementing coding for your marketing team, edge workers might be what you're looking for

    iii)   Take an inventory of all the different tools that you're using in both marketing and sales, and rationalize your martech stack

    iv)   Stay on top of how you can use martech to transform the way that your marketing strategy is implemented

    v)   Optimize your systems and your automation flows, and centralize your reporting

    vi)   Automate as much as your reporting, bidding and analysis that you can to free up more of your time, to focus in on areas where you can add a lot more value

    vii)   Review all of the tasks that you do manually on a regular basis and try to automate them, allowing you to focus on more creative tasks

4

SITE STRUCTURE, SEO & VOICE SEARCH

N ow it's time to delve into how to structure your site design, coding and content, to ensure that you create a logical, pleasing and easy-to-decipher experience for both users and bots alike – not focusing too much of your time and energy on just the one over the other.

33) Does your website pass the website content accessibility guidelines with the WCAG? Jeff White

Jeff White, Founder of *KulaPartners.com* starts off this chapter with a challenge for you: "Do you know if your website passes the website content accessibility guidelines with the WCAG?"

"Most people don't even know what that is, let alone if their website is designed and maintained to be accessible. If that's you, what you may not realise is that you may actually be breaking the law in your country, or in countries that your website serves if your site is not accessible. It would be no different than if you owned a restaurant and it didn't have a wheelchair ramp.

"In 2018, the number of lawsuits that were filed against companies with inaccessible websites was approximately 30% higher than the year before – and there were 470 cases filed in Q3 of 2018 alone. These are really high-profile lawsuits with potential brand implications and other related problems for website owners.

"In the US, nearly 13% of the population has a disability. This accounts for around 25 million people! They may have a visual or auditory impairment, or mobility or cognitive disabilities.

"While there's never been a better time for assistive technologies like screen readers, which are being built into many devices these days, the fact is that if your website isn't built to the level of the WCAG 2.0 guidelines or better, the assistive technologies can't help.

"You may actually be breaking the law in your country, or in countries that your website serves if your site is not accessible."

JEFF WHITE
@brightwhite

"In reality, complying isn't even that hard to implement. Some of the easiest measures include things like ensuring that your image content has appropriate descriptive alt tags (alternative text for blind users). You can have captions on your videos and transcriptions of your audio content to ensure that deaf users can consume your content too. You should also ensure that there's plenty of contrast in your website design so that your headlines stand out against the background colour.

There are official guidelines for all of these requirements. These standards should be so easy to accomplish.

"Some of the more difficult elements that you might require a web developer for include making sure that your site is fully accessible via keyboard browsing so that you don't have to use a touch-type device in order to find your way around the site. Any competent developer should be able to keep you on the right side of the law here.

"To summarise, my actionable tip is that you talk to your web design agency today, and make sure that your site is already set up to be accessible – and if it's not, fix it. Doing so doesn't just mean that millions of disabled users will be able to use your site, buy from you or enjoy your content – it might just keep you out of court too!"

34) Image SEO, international SEO & information architecture - Gianluca Fiorelli

Our next expert, Gianluca Fiorelli from *iLoveSEO.net* approaches coding, content and design from an SEO perspective. Gianluca says: "I have three quick tips. And the first one is all about image search…

"Pinterest led image search, then came Bing, and over the past year or so Google has been pushing and reinventing Google Image Search. One of the most interesting things that they have done recently is to position Google Lens inside image search in the U.S.A.

"This is likely to spread to Google in other countries – so my first tip is to rediscover Google Image search, and rediscover SEO for image search, because everything we have loved about Pinterest search is going to be possible on Google in the near future. This also relates to what is going to be a magical combination between voice search and visual search, which I think is going to be massive over the coming years.

"My second tip is for anyone working on international SEO, and that's to stop thinking that your job is done, as soon as you implement HREFLANG.

"Keeping going, fully localising your website to give a truly regionalized experience for the people viewing your website from all the countries that you're targeting. Don't leave everyone around the world devouring the same content. Because an Italian is interested in different things compared with a Spaniard, an American or a Brit. Work with your developers to evolve a really agile CMS, so that you can implement all of the local content changes that are going to benefit you and your site.

"Everything we have loved about Pinterest search is going to be possible on Google in the near future."
GIANLUCA FIORELLI
@gfiorelli1

"Thirdly, make sure that your information architecture is optimal. Good information architecture – i.e. website navigation, is the best way to ensure that Google, and your users find it easy to navigate through your site. At the same time, review your taxonomy (how you choose to categorize your website content) to make sure that it's as logical as possible for both users and search engines alike."

35) Deliver a mobile-friendly user experience - Paul Lovell

For Paul Lovell from *AlwaysEvolvingSEO.com*, creating a mobile-friendly user experience is key to present-day marketing success. Paul says: "My actionable tip is to design your site with mobile indexing and page speed in mind.

"Google rolled-out their mobile-first crawling update in March of 2018, after about a year-and-a-half of testing. However, a lot of the big e-commerce sites are still not mobile-friendly to users. They're still using clunky desktop sites, with mobile device users often still having to pinch and zoom to view the content.

> *"Some of the bigger e-commerce sites could speed their home page up by around two seconds, just by compressing their images."*
> **PAUL LOVELL**
> *@_PaulLovell*

"These are businesses with big marketing teams and big budgets that are still not moving with the times. Google are gradually trying to force them in the right direction. At the moment, the brand authority of these big businesses is ensuring their continued success, but that's not going to last forever. Unless they start creating experiences that are designed for the mobile user, smaller, niche businesses are going to take over.

"My second tip is page speed. This became a Google ranking factor in July 2018 and again, big businesses are falling behind here. Many sites still haven't taken care of something as simple as compressing their images. Research that I've done recently shows that some of the bigger e-commerce sites could improve the speed that their home page loads by around two seconds, just by compressing their images.

"Back in March 2018 Google conducted some related research and they found that if you could improve your page load speed by 2 seconds, this could increase conversion rates by 15%. That should be a massive financial win for any business!"

36) Mobile-first indexing - Bridget Randolph

Another top SEO who's keen to encourage marketers to take advantage of Google's mobile-first indexing is Bridget Randolph from *WheelhouseDMG.com*. Bridget says: "If you're not feeling super-confident with what mobile-first indexing is and what it means for your business, now is the time to find out.

"Essentially, mobile-first indexing means that Google is starting to treat the mobile version of your website as the primary version – which means that if your content isn't published on your mobile site version, Google won't consider it when it comes to determining where to rank your pages.

"However, don't panic – you're probably OK! We've been talking about mobile SEO and mobile websites for years now, and most people are doing a lot of good things with that.

"If you've kept up with good practice responsive web design, or just ensured that you're delivering a good mobile site experience, you probably don't have too much to worry about. Google are rolling this algorithm update out very slowly, just to make sure that everyone's in a good place.

"So don't panic, but do start looking at your current mobile site experience, and making sure that it's a really good experience for your visitors. Because increasingly, people are going to discover you on the mobile web, rather than on a desktop.

"The key thing is to make sure that everything that you want people to see on your website is available from the mobile version – because way back, when we first started doing mobile-friendly versions of our websites, we told people to keep it light, keep it to the minimum of what you need your audience to see on a phone. If you listened to that advice, your mobile site might look different compared with your desktop version.

"Google are now saying that your mobile site version is going to be considered as your primary version, so if you want your content to be seen, make sure it can be experienced on your mobile site version.

> *"Make sure that everything that you want people to see on your website is available from the mobile version"*
> **BRIDGET RANDOLPH**
> *@BridgetRandolph*

"In relation to your site versions, I'd also like to highlight something called switchboard tags. These are tags that are similar to canonical tags, but switchboard tags tell Google which version of your site (i.e. desktop or mobile) it should consider as the primary version.

"People ask me if they have their desktop site version set up as their primary site, whether or not they should be changing this. What I'm saying right now in response to that is 'no'. Google are saying that if that's the way that you currently have your site set up, stick with it. Don't change that just for the sake of mobile-first indexing.

"To summarise, if you've been ensuring that your visitors have a good mobile experience, you should be fine. But now is a great time to double-check, making sure that you are in a good place, and that your user-experience is really solid, and that you're not missing anything on your mobile site that you want both users and search engines to discover."

37) Keep on testing your site speed - Pam Aungst

As Paul Lovell highlighted, improving your page speed enhances your user experience. And this is something on which Pam Aungst from *PamAnnMarketing.com* builds upon. Pam says: "Google wants your sites to load faster. They've been talking about this for a long time, since around 2009. In 2010, they incorporated page speed into their desktop algorithm as a search ranking signal. And in 2018, they incorporated it as a mobile ranking signal as well."

"A lot of marketers are aware of this by now, but the recent twist is that when Google announced the mobile search algorithm update in January 2019 and said it was coming six months later and then implemented it in July, a lot of marketers were using Google's PageSpeed Insights tool to test their site's speed on mobile and desktop.

> *"Start doing what you can to optimize your site for a really slow mobile speed."*
> **PAM AUNGST**
> *@PamAnnMarketing*

"That's all well and good, but at the time, that tool only tested for the presence of page speed optimization best practices and not your actual page speed – not the actual number of seconds it takes for your website to load. Actual page load time is supposedly, at least in part, what Google uses in its ranking algorithm.

"Additionally, website owners should be aware that the new version of PageSpeed Insights uses the engine of a tool called Lighthouse, which emulates a 1.6 megabits per second connection for the mobile test. That is extremely slow compared to the cellular internet connection that most of us have and use.

"In the US, most people use Wi-Fi on their mobile devices, so that means that they have an average mobile connection speed of 18 or 19 megabits per second. On the mobile internet in much of the United States, you're still going to get in the region of 12-13 megabits per second, but Google still wants you to optimize your sites for just 1.6 megabits per second. This is really hard to achieve!

"The important thing to bear in mind is that, in preparation for the mobile speed algorithm update, you might have used the earlier version of the PageSpeed Insights tool and thought that you were doing OK in terms of mobile site speed. However, you may be rather unpleasantly surprised if you test again using the new version of the tool! So, re-test your site regularly using PageSpeed Insights and start doing what you can to optimize your site for a really slow mobile speed."

38) Don't just focus on individual pages when testing loading speed - Marcus Miller

Something else to bear in mind when it comes to speeding up your site is the importance of testing lots of different page types, not just your home page. This is a tip brought to you by Marcus Miller from *BowlerHat.co.uk*.

Marcus says: "Optimizing loading speed is nothing new, but it's crucially important. Every marketer knows the importance of your page loading speed. Fast sites improve your SEO and boost conversion rates – so in theory, improving your page loading speed can add value to all your digital marketing activities.

"The problem we see is how marketers approach page speed optimization. Typically it's done once and then forgotten about, or it's done only on key pages like the home page, and then not monitored over time.

"What we see in the real world is that the majority of pages load more slowly than the pages that have been optimized. We saw this ourselves on our BowlerHat blog where a few of our most popular blog posts were taking around three times longer than the site average. Not cool!

"We also had a client for which we optimized their home page, and the very next day they uploaded an eight megabyte background, which completely tanked the loading speed! Fortunately, there's a free tool which the majority of site owners already have installed which can help them monitor and improve page speed across their the entire site – and that's Google Analytics.

"What you should be doing in Google Analytics is going to the 'Behaviour' section and then clicking on the 'Site Speed' report. There are three parts to the Site Speed report. Firstly, the Overview section. This provides a general overview of page loading speeds alongside DNS and web hosting stats – all actionable items that can improve your site performance.

"Page speed optimization is not a fix-and-forget job."
MARCUS MILLER
@marcusbowlerhat

"Next, go to 'Page Timings', my favourite report in this section of Google Analytics. Here we have a list of all the pages on your site, ordered by page views, so you see the pages that get the most traffic. Next to that is a column that shares the relative loading speed of each page. This is where you can identify important pages that aren't loading as fast as the pages that you've already optimized.

"The third report in this section of GA is the 'Speed Suggestions' report. This report works in conjunction with

Google PageSpeed Insights. Here you can obtain specific feedback on what you can do to improve each and every page.

"The first key takeaway from these tips is that page speed optimization is not a fix-and-forget job. You can optimize something, and the very next day something else can go wrong. Or you can optimize the global elements of your site and find that other elements on individual pages are bringing the speed of those pages down.

"The second key takeaway is that page speed needs to be reviewed across the entire site. And the third takeaway is that Google Analytics is a free tool that enables you to review page speed across your entire site in five short minutes.

"Dive into your analytics, review all major page types (home page, product pages, category pages and blog posts) and then review all of your major pages individually. After that, keep monitoring this over time, testing your major pages and reviewing your speed stats inside of Google Analytics."

39) Improve your on-site SEO using Google's dynamic search ads - Jason Barnard

Another man who's using Google's software to continually improve the performance of his site is Jason Barnard, founder of *Kalicube.pro.*

Jason says: "Over the past year I've been testing using dynamic search ads by Google Ads. I've been using the organic index to optimize my campaigns in Google Ads.

"For dynamic search ads, Google chooses the headline, the search query, and the landing page. All you need to do is write descriptions for your extensions and Google will do the rest. What's really nice about this is that you feed Google the pages that you want to use in your paid campaigns from your successful SEO pages.

"After a few hours, or a few days of your paid campaign, you can see how Google is misinterpreting your SEO inside Google Ads. That's amazing! Because instead of waiting for a couple of months, you can get the information within a couple of days or hours, depending on the size of your company.

"You can see where Google gets the headlines wrong, where it's getting the landing page to search query relationships wrong. Then you should go back to your SEO and correct the errors. Use the insight gained from your paid campaigns to optimize your organic titles, meta descriptions and headlines. If Google hasn't understood your landing page correctly, you need to improve that.

> *"You can see how Google is misinterpreting your SEO inside Google Ads."*
> **JASON BARNARD**
> *@jasonmbarnard*

"After a few days of running your paid campaigns, go back and correct your SEO, wait a couple of more days, get more data and do it again. Throughout the process you should be making money from your AdWords campaigns, and using the data you receive in those campaigns to improve your SEO.

"After a while, you've got this really nice on-page SEO, which is being helped by profitable paid campaigns, assuming you set a sensible target CPA. As well as your paid campaigns getting better over time, your SEO's improving too. I find that fascinating!

"Over time you've got this really nice cycle going on. After a while, once you've got perfect on-page SEO and you've got perfect ad campaigns running.

"It takes a little bit of time, but then you can turn your efforts to improving your UX and your sales funnel, which will push the conversion rate up and improve performance of both organic and Google Ads – and of course improvements in conversion rates benefit every other channel."

40) Steal your competitor's featured snippets - Stephan Spencer

From taking learnings from your paid campaigns to improve your SEO, let's move on to taking learnings from your competitors to improve your SEO, with Stephan Spencer from *StephanSpencer.com*.

Stephan says: "My top tip is to leverage the power of featured snippets – and stealing featured snippets from your competitors is one of the easiest ways to get that coveted position zero!

> *"Stealing featured snippets from your competitors is one of the easiest ways to get that coveted position zero!"*
> **STEPHAN SPENCER**
> *@sspencer*

"Imagine having a top competitor that has thousands or tens of thousands of featured snippets. The way that you would discover this is by going to a tool like SEMrush, researching your competitor's domain, clicking on the 'Organic Research' tab and then selecting 'Featured Snippets'.

"When you have a list of your competitor's featured snippets, what you need to identify is which of these snippets are the easiest prey to go after! To do this, you need to determine which snippets are in the wrong format.

"For example, let's say that you were considering the search query 'How to boil an egg.' It's best to answer that sort of query in a numbered-list format. If a paragraph snippet is being used for this sort of query instead, that's not the optimal readable format. If you aim for the optimal format, as well as giving yourself a better opportunity to rank as the featured snippet, you'll also be likely to be chosen as a voice search answer.

"I should mention that you should be doing this work on your own domain too. Do analysis to discover all your own featured snippets, determine how weak or strong your answers are, and reduce the chances of somebody else stealing your snippets."

41) Focus on domain authority - Justin Champion

To increase the chances of your content ranking highly in the SERPs, you should also be focusing on trying to improve the overall domain authority of your site, according to Justin Champion from *Academy.HubSpot.com*.

"Do some white-hat SEO with building high quality links back to your site. This will help you to improve your domain authority."
JUSTIN CHAMPION
@JustinRChampion

Justin says: "I've worked with a lot of different businesses, creating a lot of great content, and they sometimes have issues understanding why they're not getting the rankings that they're targeting. They find it hard to pinpoint the exact issue, as it takes a lot of time to produce, optimize and publish great content.

"If you're having similar issues, check out your Domain Authority score. Domain Authority essentially means how authoritative your website appears to be in the eyes of Google.

"One way of improving your website's domain authority would be to publish valuable, educational content on your site, and syndicate this content elsewhere. Something else you can do is guest post on other websites that have high authority, and build links back to your own site.

"Do some white-hat SEO, building high quality links back to your site. This will help you to improve your domain authority. It just so happens that I am working on a course on this very subject, so you can check that out over at HubSpot Academy to find out more."

42) Build links responsibly - Judith Lewis

Judith Lewis from *Decabbit.com* has some more advice on how to go about building links to your site. Judith says: "The core of search engine algorithms have been built around people finding their own way around the internet through links. I think that links have become a really dirty word, because people akin them somewhat to get-rich-quick schemes. But nothing worthwhile in life is fast, cheap and easy.

"In link building, the key message that I have been trying to get across to marketers for five or more years now is that it's about reaching out to sites that are legitimately interested in you – in the style of old web-rings, for those of you who are as old, or older than me! Web-rings allowed users to hop from site to other relevant sites, because they all offered value.

"If another website is going to link to you, why should they bother? Why should they be linking to you? You have to have some really compelling content, and I recommend to clients – and they often hate this – is that they spend a lot of time, once or twice a year, writing a really key piece of research, and using that content to reach out to other sites, and offer them a part of it too.

"Don't publish all of your content on your own site, hold something back to give to the websites that you hope are going to be linking to you. Creating value for other sites creates value for your site, giving those other sites a reason to link back to your site. They have unique content that's not on your site, and you've also got lots of great content that's not on their sites. Great organic search marketing is all about creating value for the searcher as well as the site that you're targeting to partner with.

> *"Don't publish all of your content on your own site, hold something back to give to the websites that are going to be linking to you."*
> **JUDITH LEWIS**
> *@JudithLewis*

"One day, maybe the internet will go boom, and we won't have search engines again – you never know, it could happen! If that does occur, how are we going to find our way around again? Links. If you're actively link building, please, ignore people offering you payments or payments in kind. It may sounds like a drug ad, but please build links responsibly kids!"

43) Read Google's Quality Raters' Guidelines - Marie Haynes

As Judith highlighted in the previous tip, good SEO isn't about trying to trick Google. Dr. Marie Haynes from *MarieHaynes.com* shares that Google is actually trying to help SEOs. Marie says: "What we have really taken advantage of in the last year or so is reading the information in Google's Quality Raters' Guidelines.

"These guidelines are available for everybody to read. Just search Google for 'Quality Raters' Guidelines'. They're not exactly fully descriptive of what Google is doing with their algorithms, but as Google's VP of Search, Ben Gomes recently said, they show where Google wants to go with their algorithms.

> *"Pay close attention to 'EAT' in the Google Quality Raters' guidelines, which stands for Expertise, Authoritativeness and Trust.*
> **DR. MARIE HAYNES**
> *@Marie_Haynes*

"Everybody can read them. They're about 160 pages long. It takes a few hours to get through them, but as a limited summary I would advise you to pay close attention to 'EAT' in the guidelines, which stands for Expertise, Authoritativeness and Trust.

"There's a lot of misinformation and confusion about what EAT really stands for online. It's way more than just saying, 'I'm a doctor, so my medical posts are going to be perceived as highly relevant.' The key thing is taking the time to understand how Google decides whether or not you're an authority – i.e. whether or not you have authoritative links and mentions.

"The 'T' in Google's EAT, as I've already mentioned, stands for trust. A lot of the algorithms' updates that we've seen recently in my opinion has had tons of things to do with how Google determines trust. The guidelines that Goggle have produced contain all these little hints. They talk about looking at the reputation of your business. If many of your customers are complaining online, there's a good chance that Google sees that and doesn't want to rank you highly in their results because of it.

"Google looks at things such as whether or not you have a terms and conditions page, and whether your audience can easily find how to get a refund from you. What we've seen is that a lot of sites that were hit with recent algorithm updates had issues that are directly outlined in the Quality Raters' Guidelines as trust issues.

"Finally, there's a lot of information in the Quality Raters' Guidelines about ads and ad quality too. They talk about things such as if you're trying to hide your ads, if you publish ads on your site. Google want to make sure that you're not trying to make any ads that you publish on your site look like the rest of your content and deceive people into clicking – that can be a sign of low quality too."

44) Why you can't just translate your sites for voice search - Michael Bonfils

Another way to improve your site's trust is to deliver a truly localized experience in every one of your target countries. This is something that Michael Bonfils from *SEMInternational.com* specialises in.

Michael says: "One of the areas that I am starting to focus on more these days is multilingual voice search. Because I do international SEO, it's not just generic voice search that I'm thinking about, but the use of voice search in a multilingual world and how we are opening ourselves up to a new era of misunderstanding".

"For example, A lot of marketers or site managers just use translation tools – i.e. Google Translate or something like that. Some site owners just translate their site FAQs.

"With voice search, if you're in Sweden and you ask, 'What's wrong with my laptop, Alexa', you're going to get a response that's appropriate for where you are in the world and the answer might be wrong.

"If the localised versions of your websites are just auto-translated or translated by a translator who does not understand search intent, you may be missing out on many opportunities. It's time to look at all of your multilingual campaigns, and make sure that they're written by local search experts, or by people who are local to the ground. Your writers need to understand the local culture, and the language. And most importantly, they need to understand how searchers use voice differently compared with when they're typing in searches.

"If the localised versions of your websites are just auto-translated or translated by someone who does not understand search intent, you may be missing out on many opportunities."
MICHAEL BONFILS
@michaelbonfils

"As a funny example... A long time ago, I was dating this Hungarian girl. I had learned a little bit of Hungarian translating things from our English language to theirs. I was going to meet her father for the first time. I went to her place. She opened the door and her father was standing there. I introduced myself, 'Bonfils Michael I am.' He responds, 'Oh.' He said his name. Then he said, 'Hogy vagy?,' which means, 'How are you?'. Now, because it was hot, I stated the directly translated word, 'Meleg.' Then he looked at his daughter, patted her on the back and said, 'Good job, this guy's perfect for you.' I'm like, 'That was weird.' Then she's trying not to laugh. I sit down, and I ask, 'What is so funny?' She goes, "Meleg' does mean hot, but it also means when you are using it to describe how you feel, you just told him that you're gay!'

"Remember, people also search with a longer-tail phraseology when using voice. Sometimes when you talk to people in different cultures, they'll mix English with their own language because it makes it easier to articulate what they're trying to say. In Panamanian Spanish, people might say 'raspberry' instead of the correct Spanish word for raspberries. There are all of these idioms to be aware of and each country and language is different.

"In Sweden, they frequently mix English with Swedish during a conversation. Often because it's easier to say the English word than the Swedish one. These considerations are very important to be aware of as an international search marketer. It is therefore recommended that you build your discovery strategy around native voice. Preparing for voice search internationally is something you should be thinking about now if your business crosses borders in any way."

45) How voice is changing the way we search - Alex Moss

Alex Moss from *FireCask.com* continues with the voice search theme, exploring how voice search is changing user behaviour. Alex says: "I could probably extend onto what Michael shared in the previous tip, because I've been exploring the Medic Google algorithm update a lot recently. Note that the Medic update isn't just about content – it's also about relevancy from the searcher's intent.

"What I'm seeing is that there are more long-tail keywords and there is more search intent to voice searches compared with text-based searches.

"My top tip would be to look at the way that your site architecture works and the way in which you're delivering answers to whatever your target market is searching for.

"If someone searches for "How do I fix my laptop?', that's intent. You have to deliver on that requirement. Instead of just having a generic page, trying to rank for related keyword phrases, the next generation of content marketing should evolve into providing answers to specific queries.

"It feels like we've been hearing about voice search for several years now, but it also feels like voice search is finally now relevant to the mainstream consumer – and that's significant for marketers.

> *"Children tend not to type into search engines nowadays. Instead, they're asking Amazon Echos or Google Home devices"*
> **ALEX MOSS**
> *@alexmoss*

"I heard a talk at an event recently where the speaker said that over the next year, voice search will overtake native typing searches. Someone in the audience said, 'That's rubbish.' I told this story to a friend at a dinner party – he had nothing to do with marketing – and he said, 'I completely agree and I'm actually surprised that it's not happened sooner.' The difference between those two people is that my friend at the dinner party had children. He said that children tend not to type into search engines nowadays. Instead, they're asking Amazon Echos or Google Home devices – and they already have a specific intent behind their search.

"In the past, we laughed at our grandparents with black and white TVs. Now, we've reached a point where typing search phrases into Google will become the black and white TVs of SEO. Our kids will be incredulous that we ever had to manually type something into a search engine!"

46) How big is the voice search opportunity? - Mitch Joel

Mitch Joel from *SixPixels.com* would like to emphasise that voice search is happening in volume right now. Mitch asks: "What will your brand voice strategy and your unique positioning be in this world? As Alex touched upon in the previous tip, Gartner shows that around 30% of all searches are going to be conducted without a screen in the next two years.

"Close to 60 million adults in the USA currently own one form of smart speaker. There's a billion devices that provide voice assistant access today and search is going to be a big driver of this.

"However, to me, what's more important is what's your actual brand voice strategy? What does your brand voice sound like? Is it going to be a talent? Is it going to be a celebrity? What gender is it going to be? How are you going to evoke and tell stories in this new medium?

"Right now, this whole bucket that I call smart audio isn't really interactive. You ask it a question, it responds and then the discussion dies at that point. But it's going to start asking you questions back soon.

"We're going to get to a point where AI can really mimic the voice, and be somewhat responsive and conversational. The ability to tell stories and participate in that Q&A directly with consumers is going to be massive. Some marketers say, 'How huge? Is this all hype?' I don't believe it is. From what I've seen and heard, Amazon Alexa's team is 10,000 people right now. This is real, and it's growing fast.

"The business models aren't really there yet. We don't know how voice search going to be monetized yet. This may be done through keywords, invocations for voice search and how you invoke the device to tell you what you want. Perhaps the device's answers will be ranked the same way that a Google paid ad might be?

"Alexa, which is dominating the space right now, is considering some kind of subscription model. We may be looking at a conversion-based way to monetize this. The rules haven't been set yet but this doesn't mean that now isn't the time to move in and take advantage of this rapidly emerging technology.

> *"30% of all searches are going to be conducted without a screen in the next two years"*
> **MITCH JOEL**
> *@mitchjoel*

"I see this as early days of land grab. Think about SEO back in the day, or think about domain grabbing back in the day – that's exactly where we're at with smart audio.

"Right now, if you use these devices, they're great, but it's a barren landscape. There's not a lot of great content available through them yet and that's a huge opportunity for marketers – especially if you can combine your voice results with a really compelling talent to make this opportunity work for your brand."

47) Voice is going mainstream alongside smarttech - Nick Wilsdon

Just to make sure that you are left in no doubt as to whether or not voice search deserves a significant part of your attention in this new marketing world, Nick Wilsdon from *NickWilsdon.com* highlights how voice search, blended with smarttech is changing the marketing game.

Nick says "You can see that Amazon and Google are fighting for market share in voice at the moment. The big change that's happened recently is that they've both released their chip set, the technology – and that's now going into different smart devices.

"Voice assistants are going to change the whole way we do marketing."
NICK WILSDON
@nickwilsdon

"Amazon has put proof of concept into a microwave. Google is releasing their technology for new Panasonic TVs. We're going to see an absolute explosion in the number of devices that have smart technology in them for relatively little cost. This way, manufacturers can differentiate their products by making them smart.

"Research that Gartner shared in 2017 suggested that 75% of U.S. households will have smart devices by the end of 2020 – I think that may actually prove to be a conservative estimate. With this chip set explosion the percentage could be even higher. A large audience is coming to this revolution, rapidly.

"Think about how can you get ready for this change as a brand. Something that I would suggest that you focus on is how to make your information services machine readable and use that to stake your claim to a share of Alexa Skills and Google Actions.

"Consider how you run this automatically from your website with Schema and microformat markup. Think about how you can make as much of your content as possible accessible to this new technology. For marketers, this probably involves a different way of thinking. Firstly you should be focusing on

Schema deployment; and then, prioritising anything that involves making information available and understandable to these devices.

"Overall, voice assistants are going to change the way we do marketing. We're going to move from SEO being something that's primarily focused on Google and the Google SERPs to SEO being about discovering – allowing our brands to be discovered in all these different environments. Voice is going to be a big game changer for SEO as well as marketing in general."

48) Schema for voice search - Jonny Ross

But how do you actually start to make voice search work for you right now? As Nick Wilsdon touched upon in the previous tip, the key for Jonny Ross from *Fleek.marketing* is that you help search engines to understand the context of your content, using Schema.

Starting off from where Alex Moss finished in tip 45, Jonny says: "If you look at younger generations, more and more people are using voice search. And the reason behind that is that we can talk three times faster than we can write.

"There's also a great opportunity to be in Google's answer box – position zero; right at the top of Google for lots of different queries. Google's answer engine powers voice search.

"You should be thinking about what your target market is searching for and how they are searching – i.e. using longer questions. To take full advantage of this, one of the key elements is the use of Schema, marking up as much of your content as possible with code that tells Google precisely what your content means.

"Whether you're a dentist, a vet or a radio station, there's all sorts of different Schemas – there are thousands of Schemas.

Currently I'm doing a lot of work with job websites and recruitment agencies. Google are currently pushing their jobs board, and so we're marking up lots of job listings with Schema to appear high in Google's search results.

"Recently, I've been getting lost in standard occupational classification taxonomies, which if you're interested and you're doing job Schema, have a look at O*NET SOC taxonomy. There are 974 different job types that have a code next to them. If you use the right code in your Schema, that's a great way of ensuring that you get your content seen in the right place within Google Jobs.

> *"Never forget that giving great customer service is great marketing too"*
> **JONNY ROSS**
> *@jonnyross*

"However, don't get too lost in the technical details and forget the big picture either. Nothing radical has changed about best practice marketing in years. It's still about ensuring really good customer service.

"Keep returning to your customer journey. Provide delight, give surprises; determine what your customers might not be happy with. Think about how you can turn some of your bad customer experiences around and never forget that giving great customer service is great marketing too."

Chapter 4: Site Structure, SEO & Voice Search – summary

i)   Make sure that your website passes the website content accessibility guidelines with the WCAG, otherwise you could be breaking the law

ii) Start giving a truly regionalized experience to the people viewing your website from all the countries that you're targeting

iii) Design your site for mobile indexing and fast page speed to improve user experience and enhance discoverability

iv) Google is starting to treat the mobile version of your website as the primary version, which means that if your content isn't published on your mobile site version, they won't consider it – make sure that Google can crawl your content from the mobile version of your site

v) Optimize your site for a really slow mobile speed to ensure that your site is classified as a fast site by Google

vi) Monitor and improve your page speed across your entire site using Google Analytics

vii) Use Google Ads to see how Google is misinterpreting your SEO, and then use that information to improve your SEO

viii) Steal featured snippets from your competitors to get that coveted position zero

ix) Track your domain authority over time and aim to continually improve it, increasing the likelihood of your content being discovered

x) Provide value for sites that you want to link to your own site – consider offering them high quality, unique, free content in exchange for that link

xi) Pay close attention to 'EAT' in the Google Quality Raters' guidelines, which stands for Expertise, Authoritativeness and Trust.

xii) Beware of local idioms when preparing for voice search internationally

xiii) Publish content that meets a searcher's intent – this supersedes focusing on trying to optimize your pages for target keyword phrases

xiv) Decide on your brand voice strategy. What does your brand voice sound like? What will the voice sound like? Is it going to be a celebrity? What gender is it going to be? How are you going to evoke and tell stories in the world of voice search?

xv) To get prepared for voice search, think about Schema deployment and then prioritise anything that involves making information available, whether it feeds the Schema or any of these related technologies

xvi) Keep returning to your customer journey. Provide delight, give surprises; determine what your customers might not be happy with. Think about how you can turn some of your bad customer experiences around – and never forget that giving great customer service is great marketing too

We've covered a great deal in Technical Success: the first part of Marketing Now. Before proceeding to Creative Success, part 2, watch the first of our three free video workshop recordings, pinpointing how specific businesses can implement the tips shared in this book. Sign up to watch the video at *DavidBain.com/MarketingNow*.

PART 2:
CREATIVE SUCCESS

5

USER EXPERIENCE & CUSTOMER EXPERIENCE

From site structure to SEO and voice search in the previous chapter, it's now time to move onto the impact that these technical improvements can have on your user experience – and how to ensure the optimal customer experience.

49) Stop selling products and start selling experiences - Ben Tepfer

Ben Tepfer is a Global Technical Evangelist for *Adobe Experience Cloud*, and *Adobe Experience Platform*, and believes that creating memorable experiences is the way to build a long-term, committed customer base.

Ben says "I would encourage you to stop selling products and start selling experiences. We use this phrase a lot here at Adobe – it's referring to how you differentiate yourself as a business in the marketplace today.

"Customers remember a great experience. They remember going into a store and having a unique moment with a sales representative who truly engaged with them. In the same way, they remember when they go to a website and they receive a personalised, tailored experience, that assists them and drives them towards an informed purchase decision.

"Here at Adobe we did a study over the past year that found that businesses that focus on both selling and creating customer experiences generate more revenue – so it's actually good for the profitability of your business to invest in these experiences.

> *"Businesses that focus on selling and creating customer experiences generate more revenue"*
> **BEN TEPFER**
> *@bentepfer*

"To go alongside that, I'd also like to emphasise the impact of surprising and delighting your customers. I'm seeing more and more brands creating personalised experiences. For instance, a tailored shampoo or a personalised cologne. I remember seeing a brand send out an email with a price reduction on Black Friday, only to say that it got sent out accidentally as it contained a discount intended for employees only.

"They said something like: 'Hey, guys, we're closing up for Thanksgiving, and don't forget to use your employee discount this week!' They made it *look* like the email was just intended for internal recipients, but actually, it was a promotional email, intended on making customers think that they were getting an additional discount that wasn't supposed to be made available to the general public.

"If you followed the discussion about the promotion online, you could have seen that tons of consumers were saying things like, 'Hey, I think you got this wrong!' However, when customers used the code, and it worked, the surprise and delight it created was really impactful.

"As we move forward as marketers we need to think a lot more about how we differentiate our propositions through these exciting and different experiences, then how we create these memorable moments that our customers come back time and time again for, sharing their experience with their own communities."

50) Make sure your website content is readable - Steve Linney

Another way to create a better customer experience is to make your website more readable, and that's what Steve Linney, Marketing Manager for *TheSecurityBureau.com* is focused on.

Steve says: "If a web page doesn't load within three seconds, and it's not readable within 10 seconds, visitors leave and they then look for a faster and clearer experience. You have around 7 seconds to grab someone's attention once your web page has loaded.

"Poor website readability is a sign that you're not looking after your audience. What this can mean is you are spending a lot of time, money and resources producing content that's not fit for purpose.

"If you don't have an engaged audience, you lose audience trust and you find that your customers are taking their business elsewhere. Ultimately, you lose revenue.

"One good way to look at it is if you want your content to be understood by 80% of Americans, write at grade eight level. A lot of online content doesn't do this. It's too complex for the average consumer.

"This is something that the Dutch Government also found when they began to use readability tools. They found that their content was too complicated for the majority of readers in the Netherlands.

> *"If you want your content to be understood by 80% of Americans, write at grade eight level."*
> **STEVE LINNEY**
> *@stevelinney*

"Without the clarity that good readability brings, you can cause a lot of problems for your customer as well as yourself. So much so, having good readability is becoming a recognised legal requirement. We've seen this happen in Texas, where car insurance documents now have to be at a minimal readable standard to be legally valid.

"We collect readability data from clients such as NASA and Shopify, and we found a few common issues like the overuse of long sentences, too many adverbs, buzzwords, geek-speak, jargon and acronyms.

"There's also the use of long words when simple words will do. And there's often confusion between formal and conversational tone.

"The good news is that these mistakes can be avoided by adopting readability measures as part of your content assessment process. Having content that's readable helps to deliver the clarity of your message. It's not about dumbing-down what you're saying. You're simply making sure that the largest number of people can understand what you're trying to communicate.

"A good quote that I like to use by Bernard Kilgore – who was Editor of the Wall Street Journal – says 'Write from the expert, but write so that the non-expert can understand.'

"Here's another tip… Having a short video at the top of your written content helps too. This means that you have the written content on the page, but then you also have a video, another way of consuming the content that engages the consumer, keeping them on the page for longer."

51) How to direct visitors once they're on your site - Shelley Walsh

Someone else who understands the value of knowing how best to deal with traffic when it lands on your site is Shelley Walsh from *ShellShockUK.com*.

Shelley says: "If you produce and publish content, you should also be focused on what visitors do once they visit your site. A lot of marketers don't focus enough attention as they should on this – focus tends to be spent on getting the traffic, rather than keeping the traffic.

"You should also be concentrating on what experience the user is going to have once they're on your page. Don't deliver a non-relevant content nightmare such as a page that doesn't answer your visitor's question or query. A dead-end page, badly written and badly presented is my absolute worst no-no.

"Another bad example is where a page has no relevance to the SERP (search engine results page), or the link that visitors came through. This often results in what's called a fast bounce and no return to the site from the visitor.

"I would suggest that you first spend your time understanding the psychology of your users. I read lots of books about behavioural science. I read a lot about behaviour and psychology, particularly anything by Chip and Dan Heath. I highly recommend 'Made to Stick' and 'The Power of Moments'. Also, any book by Nassim Taleb is great, as is 'Hooked' by Nir Eyal; these are all fantastic books, all focused around a similar subject.

"What you should be doing is producing content maps and experience flow maps as part of your content strategy. You can then be confident that your visitors are coming through at the right stage of the funnel for the page that they land on.

> *"Don't deliver a non-relevant content nightmare such as a page that doesn't answer your visitor's question or query."*
> **SHELLEY WALSH**
> *@theshelleywalsh*

"You should have the top of your funnel dedicated to wide queries, and the bottom of your funnel for reviews, comparisons and case studies; not the other way around. A lot of marketers are missing out on tying their content correctly to the right stage of the sales funnel.

"In addition, consider your keywords. We always come back to keywords! Pre-empt the question that the user is likely to ask at every stage of the journey and answer that question throughout the page, in every section of the page. Your page should infer to your website visitor 'this is what you're thinking', and your visitor should be thinking, 'Wow! It's like you're reading my mind!'

"Quora is a fantastic tool for discovering what an audience's questions are about a wide range of topics. Also, I find Twitter to be great for researching the questions that your target audience might want to ask. Just search for relevant topics or hashtags on Twitter – there's a wealth of information out there.

"Finally, don't forget your call-to-action. Never leave the user boxed-in. Always provide the next step. Too many marketers and web developers are ignoring this and they leave the user on a page with nowhere to go. My top tip at the moment is to focus on what visitors do on your site and to make sure that your content is of the highest quality and the utmost relevance."

52) How to meet user intent - Kevin Indig

A gentleman also focused on understanding and delivering on user intent is Kevin Indig from *Kevin-Indig.com*. Kevin says: "User intent has become so much more important in the last couple of years for marketing in general as well as for SEO.

"Look at the search results pages and the features that Google shows on the SERPs to help to understand user intent."
KEVIN INDIG
@Kevin_Indig

"User intent has always been important, but it's getting much more important. The challenge is that it's not always easy to meet the right user intent, for a couple of reasons.

"First of all, user intent is hard to identify at scale. It changes over time, so it has to be re-assessed regularly. And it's not always 100% clear. My tip is to look at the search results pages and the features that Google shows on the SERPs to help to understand user intent.

"For example, if you see that Google shows a map and a 'local pack', this strongly speaks for educational intent. A featured snippet in the answer box would indicate knowledge intent, where the searcher is trying to learn something or figure something out. If you see a shopping ad in the SERP, this indicates a transactional intent, where the user is interested in making some sort of purchase.

"Use tools such as SEMrush to pull the SERP features for different searches to understand user intent at large scale."

53) Stop sending cold traffic to a contact page - AJ Wilcox

For AJ Wilcox, LinkedIn Ads expert and Founder of *B2Linked.com*, great user experience starts with driving website visitors to the right page. AJ says: "My tip revolves around how to make sure you're providing your prospects with a lot of value, before you ever ask them to buy anything from you.

"You can implement this recommendation by publishing a free checklist offer, a free cheat-sheet, a free white-paper, or the option to join a free webinar. This isn't exactly new advice, but I still talk to companies about these sorts of things every single day.

"A lot of marketers in large organisations just haven't taken the time to understand the content game. They expect that it's possible to send cold social traffic to a contact page. It just doesn't work like that.

"It's easy to focus too much of your time and energy on the bottom of your sales funnel, trying to get people to convert. It's easy to forget that there is a much greater volume of prospects that haven't reached that conversion stage yet, but may be more likely to do so if you educate them properly and get them to know, like, and trust you.

"For business owners it's scary to go off and create, investing a whole bunch of time and money creating a great piece of content, not knowing whether it's going to work well for you. But it's an investment that you have to make.

"It's easy to focus too much of your time and energy on the bottom of your sales funnel, trying to get people to convert."
AJ WILCOX
@wilcoxaj

"One other related tip that I'd like to share – I'm a big fan of hyper-segmenting your audience. For instance, instead of saying that your target audience is marketing managers and above, split that audience into four separate groups:

i)   Marketing managers
ii) Marketing directors
iii) VPs
iv) CMOs

"When you do that, you're still going to reach all the same people, but now you have the statistics showing you which group is responding to what creative. Then, start to bid up the things that are working really well, and bid down the campaigns that aren't working so well. You can then use this data to inform you of the content that you should be writing in the future."

54) Companies that focus on monetization and retention, as well as just acquisition, are growing three times faster than companies that just focus on acquisition - Emeric Ernoult

As AJ Wilcox shared in the previous tip, focusing on delivering great, targeted user experience can result in a significant positive outcome for your business. Emeric Ernoult, Co-Founder and CEO of *AgoraPulse.com* is currently seeing significant growth in his own business, thanks to increased focus on the monetization and retention of users.

Emeric says: "Based on data, I've started to realise that companies that focus on monetization and retention, as well as just acquisition, are growing three times faster than companies that just focus on acquisition.

> *"Companies that focus on monetization and retention, as well as just acquisition, are growing three times faster than companies that just focus on acquisition"*
> **EMERIC ERNOULT**
> *@eernoult*

"I see many, many companies that focus all of their energy, budget, and people on acquiring new customers and getting more visibility, getting new leads, prospects and clients. It's fun to do that, but it's also very hard. It's probably the hardest thing to do in an ongoing, existing business.

"Companies that know how to spread their energy, resources and people across monetization – which is what you sell and how much you sell it for – as well as acquisition and retention, are growing much, much faster.

"My big piece of advice – which we're applying ourselves – is to stop focusing so much of your time and money on acquiring new customers, and start thinking on how you can monetize your existing customers better. How you can charge more appropriately for your products and services? How can you deliver more value and get more money out of your existing clients?

"Regarding retention, think about how to make sure that your existing clients stay happy and keep seeing the value in the product or service that you're providing.

"This all sounds like a 'no-brainer'. It sounds obvious and easy. But very few companies and businesses are actually doing this. We weren't doing it enough. It's not something that I see a lot of businesses spending enough time on.

"To summarize, price what you sell based on value and maximise what you sell. Most marketers start by trying to get more customers, because it's a reflex. We all think about acquiring new customers first and then retaining them. But then two years down the road we say, 'f**k our churn rate is too high! We should think about retention!' Then, four years down the road we say, 'our price is too low, we should charge more!' The funny thing is we tend to start with the acquisition piece and not think enough about the rest. The rest is the part that drives growth much, much faster; and at a much better rate than by just focusing on acquisition."

55) Connect one-to-one with your audience - Kamila Gornia

For Kamila Gornia from KamilaGornia.com, the way to shift the needle in your business is to connect on a one-to-one basis with your audience.

Kamilla says: "I really find that a lot of the more savvy consumers nowadays know what they want and know what businesses are trying to do from a marketing perspective. They know that messaging bots are being used and they know what businesses are trying to do with email marketing.

"Consumers don't connect quite as deeply as you would want when they feel that they're getting the same messages as everyone else. If you take the time to connect with somebody on a personal basis, that can help you to stand out from the crowd.

"It doesn't necessarily mean that you go out and message each of your customers on a one-to-one basis, because that might take you a thousand years! But try using something like Messenger bots to be more personable – that's a nice way to mimic a one-on-one conversation feel.

> *"Consumers don't connect quite as deeply as you would want when they feel that they're getting the same messaging as everyone else."*
> **KAMILA GORNIA**
> *@kamilagornia*

"Something else that's been working really well for us, is instead of sending a newsletter out to our entire list and asking them to sign-up to watch a webinar, instead we tell them about the webinar and ask them to reply to the email if they're interested in signing-up. Once they've replied, we send them a link.

"This obviously takes us quite a bit more time, but you can set up some automated responses that go out when people respond to you. We find that the percentage of people who respond to an email versus people that would click on a link in an email is way higher – because of that additional intrigue. They feel that they're more connected with how we're communicating.

"There's just a little bit more commitment and engagement using this approach. Think about how you can apply the same principle in your own business. Find ways to connect with your audience in a deeper way.

"Remember, it's not the size of the list that counts, it's the level of interaction that you get with your users. Looking at it from an email marketing perspective, if nobody's engaging with your messaging, you shouldn't be sending it.

"I have a lot of clients that have very small email lists, i.e. less than a thousand people. They're still making multiple six figures from their businesses. The key thing is the intimacy and connection that they have with their audience. The more it feels like their subscribers are receiving an email from a real person, the more effective that campaign's going to be."

56) Focus on getting your onboarding right - Mark Asquith

One way to build that personal relationship is to design a personalised outreach process for whenever a new customer signs-up. That's something that Mark Asquith from *RebelBaseMedia.io* believes in and practices.

Mark says: "My number one tip is get your onboarding right. If you can market and you can sell and you can create the most wonderful experience to the point that someone buys – and after that, you drop the ball, your churn's going to go up.

"Focus an incredible amount on your onboarding – the welcome sequences, the personal touches. This is something that you should integrate into the first three months of a customer using your product or service.

"If you get your onboarding right, your customers will become your fans. They'll become advocates. And you'll be able to use that advocacy for the greater good of your marketing.

If you get your onboarding right, it will directly, positively impact your bottom line.

"I see so many people getting customer onboarding wrong, because they believe that once they've made the sale that marketing stops – and it really, truly doesn't. I actually think that you've got a more difficult job in keeping customers, because we live in such a competitive marketplace. Get your onboarding right to keep your customers.

> *"I see so many people getting customer onboarding wrong, because they believe that once they've made the sale that marketing stops"*
> **MARK ASQUITH**
> *@MrAsquith*

"The cherry on the cake that I'll add to that is to do things personally that people tell you that you can't or you shouldn't be doing personally in a scalable business. Make personal, one-to-one calls. Do check-ins. Conduct audits of a customer's experience with your products or services. Be a real person with your customers. It only takes five minutes to change someone's day. Be that person and your churn rate will drop."

57) Pay attention to who else is trying to own your customer - Dixon Jones

To finish up this chapter, Dixon Jones from *DixonJones.com* brings you the concerning news that treating your own customers perfectly may not even be enough – you still might lose them!

Dixon says: "Google has stated that they're moving from sending their users to websites, to engaging with their lifetime journey. This is ultimately going to mean that they want to hold on to the customer for life. I can see Facebook, Apple and Amazon doing the same thing.

> *"We now need to concentrate on making sure that our own product, our own USP is not easily copyable."*
> **DIXON JONES**
> ***@Dixon_Jones***

"All of these big players are trying to own the customer. It's at the smaller business owner's expense. We now need to concentrate on making sure that our own product, our own USP is not easily copyable. What you produce or sell shouldn't be easy to transfer or to replicate.

"While creating and publishing content is a great way to introduce people to your product, the danger is that you're giving away your gold by giving away your content. One way of dealing with this is product differentiation – making it very difficult for competitors to match your offer.

"If you work in a content-based organisation, think about how you can make sure that you've still got premium content behind a walled garden or protected in another way. Because as soon as you give content out to the world, it's very difficult for it to bring value to you.

"We see search engines and platforms trying more and more to keep their users on their own sites and platforms – and I think that's a real long-term problem for the rest of us. Short-term, it's great, because it means we get our information out there. But for a business that wants to be around in 20 years, it's a dangerous situation to be in.

"Understand that these bodies are trying to grab your customers for life, and that your own websites are ultimately going to become less easy monetize, certainly from a knowledge-based business model perspective."

Chapter 5: User Experience & Customer Experience – summary

i)   Surprising and delighting your customers and creating great customer experiences are both likely to have a positive impact on your bottom line

ii) If you want your content to be understood by 80% of Americans, write at grade eight level – you have around 7 seconds to grab someone's attention once your web page has loaded

iii) Produce content maps and experience flow maps as part of your content strategy to be confident that your visitors are coming through at the right stage of the funnel for the page that they land on

iv) Look at the search results pages and the features that Google shows on their SERPs to understand the user intent – i.e., if you see a shopping ad in the SERP, this indicates a transactional intent

v)   Don't focus too much of your time and energy on the bottom of your sales funnel, trying to get prospects to convert – it's easy to forget that there is a much greater volume of prospects that haven't reached that stage yet, but may do if you educate them properly, getting them to know, like, and trust you.

vi) Companies that focus on monetization and retention, as well as just acquisition are growing three times faster than companies that just focus on acquisition – what are your monetization and retention strategies?

vii) Consumers don't connect quite as deeply as you would want when they feel that they're getting the same messages as everyone else – what can you do to interact with consumers on a one-on-one basis?

viii) You may find that you have a more difficult job keeping customers than finding customers in the first place, because we live in such a competitive market – get your onboarding right to keep your customers

ix) Beware that Google has stated that they're moving from taking their users to destinations, to starting to understand and engage with their lifetime journey – which ultimately is going to mean that they're going to hold on to the customer for life

6

CONTENT MARKETING STRATEGY

Let's move on to content marketing and specifically the strategy behind your approach to content marketing, which includes what content you're going to publish, who it's for and how you're going to promote it.

58) There's no prize for hitting publish - Alex Rynne

Alex Rynne from *LinkedIn.com* emphasises the importance of spending much more of your time promoting your content than you spend on creating it. Alex says: "There's too much content, but not enough effective content in the digital landscape.

"One thing that my team is really focusing on at the moment is doing fewer things, better. As content marketers we tend to launch a campaign and then move on to the next thing very quickly. We need to focus on letting our content 'breathe'.

There's no prize for hitting publish. And it's unrealistic to think that just because we publish something once and in one content format that it means that your entire audience has seen it.

"Your audience is likely to be quite diverse, with a variety of different content consumption preferences. The same consumer who prefers a 60-second video might not want to read a 50-page e-book, and vice-versa.

> *"I would recommend spending about 20% of your time creating a piece of content, and then 80% of your time distributing it."*
> **ALEX RYNNE**
> *@amrynnie*

"I would recommend spending about 20% of your time creating a piece of content and then 80% of your time distributing it. Take the time to A/B test, take the time to optimize as you go. See how your content's performing and don't forget to go back and truly measure the results before moving on to the next thing."

59) Audit your content to see how much of it is intended to attract, convince and convert an audience - Dan Knowlton

Before you get started producing your content, Dan Knowlton, Co-Founder of *KnowltonMarketing.co.uk* is keen to emphasise the importance of firstly auditing your existing content and seeing how that maps to your customer journey.

Dan says: "My number one marketing tip is to audit your current content to see how much of your content is intended to attract your audience, how much of it is designed to convince your audience and how much has been published to convert your audience.

"Consider the traditional marketing funnel, where at the top we're attracting new clients, in the middle, we're convincing those prospects that we're the right solution for their needs and then at the bottom we're encouraging them to take a call-to-action.

> *"You should be trying to answer your customer's questions before they have the opportunity to ask them."*
> **DAN KNOWLTON**
> *@dknowlton1*

"An example of awareness-based content could be educational, step-by-step tutorials. It could also be a vlog, where you're sharing storytelling content.

"When it comes to convincing those customers to buy from you, you should be thinking of all the questions that someone is likely to have if they're considering becoming one of your customers – and you should be trying to answer your customer's questions before they have the opportunity to ask them.

"The kind of questions that you should be answering at the 'convince' stage include:

- How much does it cost to work with you?
- What's the process like to become a customer?
- Do you have examples of success stories with other clients?
- What's it like to be a customer?
- What's it like to use your products?
- Are there any reviews of your products?

"Finally, for the 'convert' content... When people are ready to buy, do you make it easy for them to buy? Is it a slick process to purchase on your website? What are you doing to optimize those purchase steps?

"To summarise, my number one marketing tip is to conduct an audit to see how much awareness, convince and convert content that you have and then determine where the gaps are."

60) Spend 90% of your marketing efforts doing one thing remarkably well - Andrew and Pete

When it comes to publishing your content, should you be publishing in as many places as possible? No you shouldn't, according to Andrew and Pete from *AndrewAndPete.com*.

Andrew and Pete say: "We see that there's a lot of overwhelm in the digital marketing space. What we recommend that you do is to start following the 90-10 rule, where you spend 90% of your marketing efforts doing one thing remarkably well and 10% of your marketing efforts experimenting with everything else.

"It's getting harder and harder to stand out online. And if all you're doing is playing with new shiny things and splitting yourself across every single channel, trying to appear in as many places as possible, you're going to spread yourself too thinly. You're not giving yourself the time, the resources, the budget and the energy to do one thing really well.

"And if you do one thing remarkably well, you're going to grow so much faster than ever before. Do that one thing remarkably well first, before you branch out.

"We're not saying that you can't experiment and try new things or new ways of working. You can try repurposing your content on different platforms, but unless you're focusing on one channel, you're not going to grow as quickly as you might otherwise do. And that's the thing – we all want to grow quickly, don't we? We want to grow our audience, grow ourselves, grow our reputation. If you're spreading your efforts too thinly, you're not going to grow as fast as you possibly could.

> *"Start following the 90-10 rule, where you spend 90% of your marketing efforts doing one thing remarkably well"*
> **ANDREW AND PETE**
> *@AndrewAndPete*

"Personally speaking, our main area of focus is YouTube. It might not be the right primary channel for you, but it is for us. We love how content lasts on YouTube. It's a search engine, unlike other social platforms, where you post and then it can't be found after a few hours or a few days. We've created YouTube content years ago that's still having an impact. What's your 90% platform?"

61) Do an audit on the content that you produce and be very critical about its purpose - Bas Van Den Beld

Another man who's very clear about his intention behind the content he publishes is Bas Van Den Beld from *SpeakWithPersuasion.com*. Bas says: "I'm still seeing a lot of content on the web that doesn't serve any useful purpose – it's there because companies have set KPIs in relation to the number of articles or videos that are produced. That doesn't work. It just means that you're throwing more content out on the web, without thinking about what your target audience wants to consume.

"Consumers are increasingly more critical in choosing the content they want to see and the content they want to engage with. They have to be, because there's so much content out there. Content quality needs to be at the heart of your content strategy nowadays.

"Change your content strategy from what you might be able to rank in search engines to what's next for your audience."
BAS VAN DEN BELD
@basvandenbeld

"You should be critically analysing your content, conducting an audit at the beginning of each new year and being very critical on the purpose of each piece of content. Every piece of content should have a specific goal. If it doesn't serve any purpose, why is it there in the first place?

"This year, let's all create content that's of true high quality. You can start to do that by analysing your current content, using tools such as SEMrush, Screaming Frog and Buzzsumo to ensure that you're aware of everything that you currently have published online.

"Use these tools to see which of your content gets attention and what content doesn't. But even more importantly, review what your audience should be doing next on your site, after they've consumed each piece of content. Then change your content strategy from what you might be able to rank in search engines to what's next for your audience."

62) Consolidate your content - Brent Csutoras

Brent Csutoras also believes that a content marketing strategy should start with a thorough analysis of the content that you already have – but then the removal of 'dead wood'.

Brent says: "We're at a point where we're seeing a big transition in the internet. There are so many things that are being pulled in so many different directions. From privacy, to authority, to author profiles, video, mobile – everything.

"One of the areas that I've looked into over the last period and what I think is going to continue to be really effective, is returning your focus to the quality of your content.

"Ever since 2011, since the beginning of the Google Panda search algorithm updates, things have changed. There was a point when Google wanted to index everything on the web, but that isn't the case anymore.

"Google doesn't even want all of your good content. They certainly don't want your bad content! But the key that we've started to see is, by publishing low quality content, it makes it harder for you to rank better quality content.

"What I've seen at Search Engine Journal, and a lot of other big publications is they've taken the concept of collating 10 to 15 articles and consolidated them into one article, redirecting the old article URLs to a single core article and making sure it's current, modern and relevant.

"As a result of doing this, websites like Search Engine Journal have seen anything from 20% to 40% growth overall. All 15 pages going into one; and they're seeing from the collective traffic about a 20% to 40% boost. That's significant.

"I've seen this repeated with a lot with product sites too. Look at your analytics, and you'll almost always find that 10% or 15% of your pages are responsible for the vast majority of your website visits – and the rest of your content is doing absolutely nothing for you.

"If you look at your log files, this poorly performing content often isn't even getting indexed by search engines. We have to focus in on determining what differentiates us to build a content strategy that delivers quality.

"Also, on a related note, we're getting towards a place where over 50% of all mobile traffic no longer clicks through to a website. i.e users are getting the information that they were looking for in a different way, directly from the SERP.

> *"We're getting towards a place where over 50% of all mobile traffic no longer clicks through to a website."*
> **BRENT CSUTORAS**
> *@brentcsutoras*

"What this leads us to is having to differentiate the types of content that we're creating. Quality content should be a given, but also, as Nick and Jonny mentioned in tips 47 and 48, you have to layer Schema markup on top of your content and ensure that you're attributing authorship when and where possible.

"A lot of the current issues with the reliability of content and fact checking will be resolved over the coming years. If you're part of the solution, your content will be surfaced when appropriate, and more often.

"To summarise, scale back what you're currently doing. Stop trying to create content all of the time and focus on creating content in your space that's truly going to change the game for you."

63) Do the 'Panda' diet - Marcus Tandler

Someone else who encourages you to scale back the quantity of your existing content is Marcus Tandler from *Ryte.com*. Marcus says: "My tip is for you to do the 'Panda' diet. In the age of Google's Panda algorithm updates, index bloat is a definite threat. Millions of indexed HTML documents are not an asset, but a liability. Indexing everything is inefficient by definition. Most of your website is usually dead weight, and it's pulling down your best pages.

> *"Most of your website is usually dead weight, and it's pulling down your best pages."*
> **MARCUS TANDLER**
> *@mediadonis*

"For every URL you have, you should ask yourself three questions:

i)   Do I need this page for my users?
ii) Does this page need to be indexed?
iii) Does this page need to rank for something?

"This way, you will get rid of useless category and tech pages, faceted search URLs (especially faceted search URLs without Google search demand), out-of-stock pages and other expired-offer pages. You should definitely set an item threshold for your pages and categories. Also, of course, get rid of other pages on your site that could be described as having 'thin content'.

"I'd like to share one more pro tip on the quickest way to remove lots of your site pages from the index – and that's to have a negative site map. I set up all the pages which are no longer needed to '410 GONE' and then built a negative site map with all of those 410 pages, submitted the site map and then I'm done. In my experience, that's the fastest way to remove lots of pages from the index. I got that tip from Joost de Valk at the last SEOktoberfest G50 Summit."

64) Focus on driving more value from your existing content - Ian Cleary

Once you're done with identifying and removing the site pages that you don't need, as per tip 62 with Brent, it's time to improve your existing content – and this is a tip from Ian Cleary from *RazorSocial.com*.

Ian says: "People always tend to focus on the creation of new content. Recently, we started to audit our existing content, evaluate it and improve it. As a result, we started to drive a lot more traffic to it. We found that you can often drive a lot more traffic to existing content than you can to new content.

"Start off by analysing which of your content isn't receiving any traffic. If it's not receiving any traffic and there's no valuable links pointing to the content, delete the content. If it's not receiving traffic and it has some valuable links, redirect it to a related post that you want to move up the rankings.

> *"Are you really using your internal links effectively enough within your site?"*
> **IAN CLEARY**
> *@IanCleary*

"Getting these additional links will help your content to move up the search rankings. Just make sure that when you're redirecting, you're redirecting to a relevant post, and that you consider adding additional, up-to-date content to the post that you want to rank higher.

"For example, I'm re-releasing a marketing tools guide this year, because I'm currently ranking well for that term. I want to maintain or improve my rankings and in order to do that I'll be editing the content, adding to the existing content, and adding internal links to the content.

"It's all too easy to forget about your existing content in the grand scheme of all of your different digital marketing activities, but it pays to do a full analysis of the content on your existing site. It's a little bit tedious, it takes a bit of time, but it's so worthwhile.

"Also, in relation to your internal links, are you really using your internal links effectively enough within your site? Look at where you're linking out to and if you want to promote some internal content, ensure that you're linking to the right posts.

"Then, start analysing the click-through rates from the SERP. Are your click-through rates really low? Maybe you can improve the meta title and description to improve click-through rates, to get more traffic."

65) Focus on building a library of content, not on building an audience - Jimmy Daly

Once you've deleted your thin content and redirected your older content to your more up-to-date, related content, what next? Jimmy Daly from *Animalz.co* suggests that you focus on building a library of content, housed on your website.

Jimmy says: "We're working with a number of B2B SaaS companies, helping them with their content marketing. The number one mistake that we see them making is running their blogs like publications.

"The term 'publication' is borrowed from a bygone era. When we look at some of our top customers, only 17 percent of their website visitors are returning visitors.

"The way that people read content nowadays is different than it used to be. Instead of trying to build an audience, which would require you to publish on a regular basis and publish on a wide range of topics, we recommend that you set aside this idea of building an audience and instead, focus on building a library of content.

"The goal then becomes to fill the shelves of your library with content on every category, and for every type of person that might read it – it's there for them when they're ready to access it.

"This does a few things. One, it treats the reader in a way that they want to be treated. It's easier for them to navigate and discover content on your site. It also facilitates a flatter site architecture. When content is more organised, it's easier for people to read and it's easier for search engines to index.

> *"We recommend that you set aside this idea of building an audience and instead, focus on building a library of content."*
> **JIMMY DALY**
> *@jimmy_daly*

"We highly recommend treating a blog like a library, slowing down your publishing cadence, going longer and deeper on the content that you create and letting go of this idea of having a regular audience.

"Building an audience will happen naturally over time as you publish great stuff. People will join your email list and follow your social channels, but this shouldn't be your primary goal.

"One great example of this approach is a company called Lattice.com, who recently organised their blog to embrace this approach. Not only are they fully practicing building a content library, they've built their site around the idea."

66) Smart content marketing strategy - Colin Gray

For Colin Gray, Founder of *ThePodcastHost.com,* when you publish content, it's important to maximise the use of that content, in many forms. Colin says: "Our big topic is 'podcasting', but we also try to do everything else around it – podcasting works best when it's supported by blogging and video.

> *"Live streaming is a great way to record a podcast."*
> **COLIN GRAY**
> *@thepodcasthost*

"Let me quickly run through our content process… We'll come up with a topic based on listener feedback, based upon queries through our website, or feedback from a real person. We rarely come up with a topic by ourselves. We then take this topic and we start writing a blog post about it.

"When it comes to producing content, I tend to start with a blog post. After writing the blog post I'll pick up the microphone and the video camera and I'll then try to record something – possibly even broadcasting it live, based upon the original blog post that I've written.

"If I'm doing a live session, I'll start off by asking the audience, 'What do you want to know about this topic?' At the beginning of the livestream I'll maybe share that I'm going to talk about the best podcast microphones, asking the audience for specific questions on the particular topic that I'm going to cover.

"If it's podcasting microphones I'm talking about, I might say, 'What podcast microphones do you currently use?' Then I'll jump straight into spending 15 minutes recording a podcast episode on that topic during the live broadcast.

"At the end of the more formal podcast recording I do some Q&A with the audience. That makes for a really good live broadcast, and livestreaming is a great way to record a podcast too. After the livestream I then chop up the video recording and publish highlights on YouTube.

"From this relatively short and simple process I've produced multiple forms of content: a blog post, a live broadcast, a podcast and video posts for YouTube. That's really smart repurposing for me. It doesn't take too long to create and tie it all together."

67) Create complementary content - Pete Matthew

Pete Matthew from *MeaningfulMoney.tv* thinks that it's important that the content you publish on different platforms isn't the same, but works together. He believes that you should be publishing complementary content.

"Don't just rely on one channel this year – publish the complementary content that your visitors need."
PETE MATTHEW
@PeteMatthew

Pete says: "What I'm doing this year, I think it's going to be massive for me and I hope that it can be massive for Marketing Now readers, is publishing complementary content.

"For instance, my audio podcast is my main content channel. That's what I spend most of my time doing. It's my 'halo' piece of content. But recently, I recorded an episode on video too.

"Maybe video is your main thing. If so, you can take the audio from your videos and publish it as a podcast. Or perhaps if you're a writer primarily, you can record your text as audio or as a video. However, producing complementary content is much more than creating multiple forms of content out of one piece.

"This year I'm creating a course, an online resource for people listening to the new season of the podcast. It will be complementary to the podcast season. Think about your customer content funnel and incorporate elements such as lead magnets and e-books where appropriate.

"Ask yourself how you can add extra value with different formats, content that your audience can consume in different ways, possibly after opting-in. Don't just rely on one channel this year – publish the complementary content that your visitors need too."

68) Refocus your content strategy on mobile - Ashley Segura

Ashley Segura from *Madhouse-Marketing.com* would like to emphasise no matter the content channel you select, you still need to appeal to the mobile user first.

Ashley says: "For a long time, we've been creating content for desktop users, which used to mean long-form content, and generally means satisfying bots more than users. From this point forward, if you haven't done so already, you need to put the mobile user ahead of the desktop user.

"I ran an experiment with SEMrush and looked at how mobile users search for keywords compared with desktop users. I looked at what sort of queries they're typing and when they land on content, how much of it they actually digest.

"It turns out that mobile users are looking for a solution that's super-fast, very actionable or trendy. Your content has to meet that need and be relevant to a mobile user's immediacy.

"When you're creating new content, you need to ask yourself whether it's likely to satisfy the requirements of mobile users by immediately providing a solution or entertainment. Or are you still just writing for desktop and burying your best content for mobile users?

"Reinvent the content that you've been creating to make it much more appealing to the mobile user."
ASHLEY SEGURA
@ashleymadhatter

"You've got to start thinking outside of what has been your content strategy and take a good look at how your target audience is discovering you and your brand today. This means learning how they're consuming your content, especially if that audience is primarily discovering your content on their mobile devices. After that, reinvent the content that you've been creating to make it much more appealing to the mobile user."

69) Your content marketing strategy doesn't have to be any more complicated than iterating a content plan - Joe Griffin

As the final piece of advice in our Content Marketing Strategy chapter, Joe Griffin from *ClearVoice.com* would like to make sure that you aren't worrying about how to create the optimum content marketing strategy before you get started.

Joe says "In my experience, you have to have an idea of your content strategy, but the important thing is to focus on creating good content for your customers instead of spending lots of time on what an overarching content strategy should look like. Just commit to a content plan.

"A content plan could be committing to publishing three pieces of content per month. Just commit to it, and do it A content strategy is a content plan that is iterated based upon results.

> *"Don't stop producing content simply because you don't have a 'pillar content strategy'."*
> **JOE GRIFFIN**
> *@joegriffin*

"Look in your analytics, iterate and get internal feedback. Don't stop producing content simply because you don't have a 'pillar content strategy'. I continually hear about marketers who get held up on the fact that they feel that they don't have the 'big content strategy'. Some people delay producing content by months, or even years because of this. They over-complicate things. Keep it simple and commit to a basic content plan. You can always grow your content strategy from there.

"So, as a business, what's the best way to go about managing this content marketing plan? The world's moving into a freelance economy. To be successful in that economy (as well as being able to identify good writers, designers and editors to hire) it's becoming increasingly important to have a managing editor to control and implement your plan.

"I would encourage companies to think about employing a managing editor. Someone who is used to managing talent and understands how to build an editorial calendar. You could have a content strategist and a managing editor, but if you can only have the one, have the managing editor who's more important from a production value perspective.

"If you just need to execute a simple content strategy, just hire someone who has experience in producing content and managing people – specifically someone who is comfortable managing freelancers. Whether we like it or not, as brands we are facing an exodus of creative talent today. The average creative person stays in an in-house position for less than 18 months.

"You have to get really good at teaching a new employee your brand voice. This is why you need a managing editor. You have to accept that this creative talent exodus that I referred to is actually occurring now and it's only going to accelerate. Prepare yourself for that reality by getting an in-house managing editor and then starting small, building freelance teams that you can work with again and again in the future, once you define your simple content plan.

"Don't get stalled by strategic thinking or selecting software to help you along the way. Just get going with defining that simple plan and using that one person in-house to execute the plan."

Chapter 6: Content Marketing Strategy – summary

i) How much time do you spend promoting your content versus creating your content? If you're not spending more time promoting your content than creating your content, you need to question how you're allocating your time

ii) Audit your current content to see how much of your content is intended to attract your audience, how much of it is designed to convince your audience, and how much has been published to convert your audience; and determine where the gaps are

iii) Follow the 90-10 rule, where you spend 90% of your marketing efforts doing one thing remarkably well and 10% of your marketing efforts experimenting with everything else

iv) You should be critically analysing your content, conducting an audit at the beginning of each new year and being very critical on the purpose of each piece of content

v) Be careful about the quality of the content you publish – by publishing low quality content, it makes it harder for you to rank better quality content in search engines

vi) Most of your website is usually dead weight and it's pulling down your best pages – for every URL that you have, determine if you need the page for your users, if it needs to be indexed and whether it needs to rank for something

vii) You can often drive a lot more traffic to existing content than you can to new content – edit existing content and build more internal links to that content

viii) Set aside the idea of building an audience and instead, focus on building a library of content

ix) Consider how you can produce multiple forms of content at the same time – maybe you livestream and record a podcast at the same time, then chop up the video and publish segments of it on YouTube

x) Don't publish the same content on multiple channels – publish complementary content

xi) Think of mobile users first when you're publishing content – this means publishing something that's super-fast, actionable and trendy

xii) A content strategy is a content plan that is iterated based upon results – don't spend too long on devising your content strategy, just commit to a content plan, and execute

7

CONTENT PLANNING, PRODUCTION & PROMOTION

As Joe Griffin shared in the previous tip at the end of chapter six, don't spend longer than you need on content marketing strategy. Get on with planning, producing and promoting your content as soon as you can. This chapter explores how you can do that.

70) Make every piece of content valuable for the consumer - Phil Pallen

Phil Pallen from *PhilPallen.expert* believes that it will hold you in great stead if you are purposeful with the use of your own time as well as being increasingly purposeful with the use of your content consumer's time.

Phil says: "In today's noisy digital environment we're inundated with messages – and marketers and consumers both need a timeout! We're seeing all sorts of people take little vacations from social media, because it's often too much to be on there every day.

"This highlights the fact that as marketers and as content creators, we need to be respectful of people's time, to make it worth their while when they're consuming our content. Don't post on social media unless you're sharing something valuable. Take everything you're writing and cut it in half. If you're sending a newsletter, get to the point! Think about how much more time you're going to reclaim when you're more efficient while you're creating.

> *"We need to be respectful of people's time, to make it worth their while when they're consuming our content."*
> **PHIL PALLEN**
> *@philpallen*

"There are a lot of marketers applying these principles effectively, but there's a guy that I've discovered in the last few months named Darius Foroux (*https://dariusforoux.com/*) who's a copywriter and a marketer. His newsletter is really amazing. I'd never even think about unsubscribing from it, because every time he emails me, it's useful."

71) When developing content, be as specific as possible - Michele Potts

Someone else who understands the value of just producing enough content to solve your consumer's needs and no more is Michele Potts from *BigSurfMedia.com*.

Michelle says "Content marketers see 7.8x more site traffic to their sites than sites that don't participate in content marketing – that's a massive upside.

> *"Be relevant, concise, and helpful with the content you produce."*
> **MICHELE POTTS**
> *@surf_big*

"However, when developing content, be as specific as possible. Be relevant, concise, and helpful with the content you produce. Provide true value for your customers and potential customers."

72) Be the best source of content in your industry - Janet Murray

And even if your content is precise, don't just publish anything that comes to mind. Janet Murray from *JanetMurray.co.uk* thinks that it's necessary to commit to being the best content producer in your industry in order to grow your audience quickly and efficiently.

Janet says: "Everyone I speak to wants to grow their audience because they want to sell their stuff, but they often don't have a big enough sized-audience to sustain the size of business that they want to create.

"However, audience growth isn't about strategies, it's about being committed to being the best content creator that you possibly can be in your space.

"When you're committed to being the best person, the go-to authority, the best source of content in your industry, you naturally build your audience, because you'll be creating really valuable, shareable content as a result of what you do. Use your marketing strategies to get your content shared. Then you'll start making a significant impact.

"Audience growth isn't about strategies, it's about being committed to being the best content creator that you possibly can be in your space."
JANET MURRAY
@jan_murray

"Marketers are often too focused on growth strategies. I.e. always asking 'How can I get more followers? How can I increase my engagement?' But if you just focus on being the best content creator and the most respected authority in your space, then you're highly likely to have a significant impact over the coming year.

"You need to show up consistently for your audience and focus on providing what they need. When you focus on them and deliver what's best for them, you'll be rewarded."

73) Remove the fear of failure - Kevin Gibbons

One challenge with content marketing is the fear of how you'll be judged. That can often lead to 'vanilla' content, content that's by-and-large the same as everyone else's content. For

Kevin Gibbons from *Resignal.com*, the key to great content marketing is to remove the fear of failure.

Kevin says: "The main challenge with content marketing is that marketers often play it too safe. They try to come up with ideas that everyone in the company is going to sign-off. However, by accepting everything that everyone says in a room, the consensus normally dilutes the idea into something that is far-removed from where you started.

"We've definitely found this in the past and I think that the biggest risk – speaking from an agency perspective – is that agencies go stale. You have to keep on innovating and improving and the only way that you can do that is by removing the fear of failure.

"One thing that we've done to combat this, is when we come up with ideas, we score them out of ten in terms of how 'crazy' the story might be able to go from a PR perspective. Obviously we want the message to be on-brand, but we don't want it to get diluted by any less than a seven in our 'crazy scale'.

"This is something that we've found has worked really well. We'll happily take the crazy scale down to an eight in terms of PR craziness. However, if PR's your goal, don't settle for anything less than a 10, because you've just got yourself into a situation where all you're doing is trying to keep everyone happy. You end up focusing on short-termism and I think that the key is to focus on what you want the outcome to be. You need to be at your most creative to achieve that. This way you're playing to your strengths and it's a strategy that's certainly benefited us.

"Another key part of this is to think of your content as a strategy, not a campaign. If you think at campaign level, you put too much pressure on trying to make it an easy-to-measure commercial success. If you think strategy, you're able to think like a VC investor, where you've got ten different companies that you've invested in. You might have four or five that are average and fail, but one or two unicorns are going to be so much better for your business than being average across the board.

"Therefore, have that mindset of not putting all of your eggs in one basket. Have the freedom to go wild with your ideas, because the best ideas are generally the most unique ones. They push what's possible.

> *"The main challenge with content marketing is that marketers often play it too safe."*
> **KEVIN GIBBONS**
> *@kevgibbo*

"Remove the fear of failure. You can still start out small and aim big, but doing content marketing this way allows you to grow – potentially faster, and with more freedom.

"Remember, when you think campaigns, you should be thinking short-term goals. Things like links, engagement and perhaps rankings. When you think strategy, you should be thinking revenue and business goals. Ultimately, if your content is going to get more buy-in from upper management, you want to be talking about making money. If you're just talking about generating links as your goals and budgets end up being cut, you're the first one to go. It's much more compelling at a higher level when you think strategy."

74) How to find content ideas - Tom Treanor

How do you come up with all of these bold, wonderful content ideas that Kevin discussed in the previous tip? Tom Treanor from *TreasureData.com* has a specific piece of actionable advice to share. Tom says: "In the modern marketing world you have to prove that you're an industry expert. You also have to get found by Google, Alexa and other voice services.

"The biggest problem that I run into when I work with different companies is that they often they have no idea what to write about. Perhaps they have enough ideas for a couple of months, but that's all. Pretty soon they're writing a bunch of 'me too' posts that are just not moving the needle. It ends up being a complete waste of everyone's time.

> *"Go to Alexa.com, register for the free trial and use it as an opportunity to fill your content marketing calendar for the next six months."*
> **TOM TREANOR**
> *@RtMixMktg*

"One actionable tip I have is to go to *Alexa.com* and subscribe for a free trial. There's a tool there called the 'Competitor Keyword Matrix'. It lets you see what all the different sites in an industry are ranking for, including your site. It also provides a 'keyword gap analysis' against your competitors. It's a wonderful place to get lots of new content ideas.

"This is the most actionable tip I can give – go to *Alexa.com*, register for the free trial and use it as an opportunity to fill your content marketing calendar for the next six months."

75) How to find keywords - Lukasz Zelezny

Another man keen to share a related, actionable tip and another tool for you try is Lukasz Zelezny from *SEO.london*. Lukasz says: "We live in a situation where there is a massive problem for organic search marketers with non-provided keywords inside Google Analytics. However, GA is immensely powerful in other areas. We also have another tool called Search Console by Google, which is another valuable tool to track your digital success.

"We have a missing gap though – and that's organic keywords. We can get some of the data we need in Google Analytics and some of it in Google Search Console. Fortunately, there is another tool that I use on a daily basis, which I highly recommend, called Keyword Hero (*https://keyword-hero.com*).

"Keyword Hero marries the data from Search Console and Google Analytics together, which is especially useful for an e-commerce business. Inside Keyword Hero you can exclude all of your brand keywords and discover the generic keywords that are driving traffic to your site and responsible for the majority of your conversions.

> *"Use Keyword Hero to get back the keyword data you thought you had lost."*
> **LUKÁSZ ZELEZNY**
> *@LukaszZelezny*

"This is a wonderful way to discover where to hone your SEO efforts moving forward. It will make your manager happier if you're working in-house. It will also make your clients happier if you work in an agency. In short, use Keyword Hero to get back the keyword data you thought you had lost and use the data that it provides to power your content marketing."

76) Stop counting words on your blog posts - Hannah Butcher

Thanks to our previous tipsters Tom and Lukasz, you're now at a stage where you know precisely what you should be writing about – but how much content is enough? There's no easy answer to that according to Hannah Butcher from *Koozai.com.*

Hannah says: "There's a lot of discussion on the web about how long blog posts should be. I've seen quite a few opinions stating that 2,000 words is a good length to aim for. My advice would be to stop counting the words in your blog posts.

"Leading marketers have previously stated that 2,000 words is this Holy Grail – in fact, Rand Fishkin recently tweeted about this. It was on a Moz blog post as far back as 2012, and it was on Search Engine Journal in 2014.

"The issue that I have with this is that we're going back to quantity versus quality. It might be that 2,000 words reads really well. But you're probably looking at examples of where people have invested a lot of time and money into creating a really great piece of content and it just happens to be around 2,000 words.

> *"If you aim for a certain word count, you'll probably just end up repeating yourself, saying the same things over and over in different ways."*
> **HANNAH BUTCHER**
> ***@HannahFButcher***

"My tip is for you to stop trying to match the word count of your competitors. I've been a freelance copywriter in the past and I had a brief spell creating blog posts that were requested to be around a certain length. In my opinion, as a professional,

I would say that most of the posts I wrote didn't need to be that length. I could probably have delivered the same quality and the same message in 600 or 700 words.

"If you aim for a certain word count, you'll probably just end up repeating yourself, saying the same things over and over in different ways.

"If you can get a post written that is naturally 2,000+ words, great. But think about your post sections, what's central to what you're trying to say, and what isn't really required.

"Keep the writing process as organic as possible. The more we artificially engineer it, the less effective it's going to be as a blog post when it's published."

77) Show your own personality in your content - Teresa Heath-Wareing

Following Hannah's point about being more free-spirited regarding the length of your content, Teresa Heath-Wareing from *TeresaHeathWareing.com* is keen that you also inject more of your own personality into what you produce.

Teresa says: "My tip is focused around list building and growing audiences. But I want you to think about this a little differently than you did in the past – specifically how you can connect with your audience through authenticity, by showing more of your personal side, so that your audience can get to know who you really are.

"Think of this in more ways than sharing on social media. Consider how you can share more of your personal side in your content, how you can show a little bit more of your personal side on blog posts or podcast episodes. At the end of the day, the main difference between you and your competitor in a huge market is little old you. You're the only thing that sets your business apart.

"For your audience to truly get to know you, you've got to show some of that personal side. And I'm going to have to take my own advice on that too, because I haven't done this a lot in the past! I've come from the corporate world where things are very professional, where you don't have personal bits involved. You and I are both going to have to change the way we do things!

> *"The main difference between you and your competitor in a huge market is little old you."*
> **TERESA HEATH-WAREING**
> *@theathwareing*

"I don't want you to think about the volume of fans or subscribers that you desire. What you need is a very warm and strong-built relationship with your audience, for people to follow you and engage with you and buy your things because you're you. Think about how you're serving that audience, how you're loving them, and how you're opening up to them from a more personal and authentic side."

78) Make sure that you incorporate stories in your content - Jessica Gioglio

One of the most effective ways to make your content more authentic and personable is to incorporate stories into it – this is something that Jessica Gioglio from *JessicaGioglio.com* suggests. Jessica says: "My actionable tip is to ensure that you're telling the stories that matter, the stories that move and motivate your audience to take action.

"The exciting thing about storytelling is that when it's done correctly, research shows that it can have a powerful effect. Stories are 22 times more memorable than facts and figures alone. Our neural activity increases by five times when listening to a story. Storytelling actually lights up the sensory cortex in the brain, allowing the listener to feel, hear, taste, and even smell your story.

> *"Stories are 22 times more memorable than facts and figures alone."*
> **JESSICA GIOGLIO**
> *@savvybostonian*

"All of this sounds good, but the problem is that for most companies, storytelling has become a bit of a buzzword, a way to support marketing campaigns or polish commercials. So much so that we often get storytelling a bit confused with content marketing.

"You need to get to the heart and soul of storytelling. The top storytellers know that storytelling isn't about projecting the desired image of your company or your products on the consumer. It's not about dropping overly-branded stories into marketing campaigns and it's not about tactics to spark consumer engagement. With more empowered customers than ever before, your brand isn't what you say it is anymore, it's what consumers say it is.

"Nowadays, capturing your customers' hearts and minds requires your business to prioritise those emotional connections when you're in storytelling mode. It requires us as marketers to be in the moment, telling stories that spark authentic conversations and to make sure that the stories we tell are relevant, moving and motivating audiences to take action. Are you ready to tell your story?"

79) Quantity leads to quality - Evan Carmichael

When and how often should you produce and publish your story? Should you take the time to hone your story before you publish, or evolve it over time as you produce and publish content? For Evan Carmichael from *EvanCarmichael.com*, the latter option is the one you should choose.

Evan says: "My actionable tip is content, more content, more content and more content! I do three YouTube videos a day. I do six Instagram posts a day. I think you need to get out there and produce more content!

> "*Quantity leads to quality. The more you do, the better you get.*"
> **EVAN CARMICHAEL**
> *@EvanCarmichael*

"If you're a thought leader, an expert or both, your voice needs to be heard more frequently. Marketers are not publishing enough content. I wish I could go to eight videos a day on YouTube. Think of yourself as a channel, not a show.

"Do the following two steps:

i)   Get good at the skill of creating content
ii)   Build the momentum necessary to stand out in your space. (I.e. produce more content.)

"How do you get to the stage where you're producing high quality content? Quantity leads to quality. The more you do, the better you get. The more you do, the more people will be talking about it. When you first start anything, you suck and the way to get better is to practise. If you go 5,000 videos in, you'll be better than when you first started. Most marketers aren't putting enough time in to become world-class at producing content.

"Expect to suck at the beginning! It's easy to look at someone else who has been producing content for a long time and think 'I can do that too!' Then you look back at your recordings and think that you're terrible and you'll never get to the top standard. Expect to suck to begin with, but that's okay. The next day you'll suck a little less!

"It took me 350 videos on my YouTube channel before I wasn't completely embarrassed by my content. 350 videos! I think that most marketers can get there faster than I did, but you need to expect to suck to begin with. If you expect to be great and then you suck, that's when you quit. If you expect to suck and then suck, you'll continue! You'll know that you're just going to get a little bit better every single day. It's the daily repetition that gets you to where you want to be."

80) Don't accept low-quality audio & visuals - David Bain

This is where my own tip fits in and if you're going to be committing to producing audio and video content on a consistent basis, commit to recording it in decent audio and video quality!

Obviously, stay authentic to the true you. As Dennis Yu advised, don't make your productions so slick that you lose the real you, but keep an eye on production quality as well. The consumer has so many choices nowadays and they'll switch off or scroll down if they can't see you or hear you well enough.

Bear in mind that in terms of content marketing, your competitors nowadays may not necessarily be who you think they are. Traditionally, your competitors are people who sell similar products and services to you, but that's not necessarily the case when it comes to maintaining the attention of today's target consumer.

Competition for attention nowadays includes the likes of Netflix and cat videos on Facebook! What value in production quality are you bringing consumers to ensure that they don't scroll down to the next thing that catches their eye? Don't give them a reason to move on to someone else!

> *"What value in production quality are you bringing consumers to ensure that they don't scroll down to the next thing that catches their eye?"*
> **DAVID BAIN**
> *@DavidBain*

As Ralph Waldo Emerson said way back in 1875, "Don't say things. What you are stands over you the while, what thunders so I cannot hear what you say to the contrary."

i.e, what you *do* speaks so loudly I cannot hear what you say.

Enhance your audio and production quality. Start by getting yourself a decent microphone, something like the 'Samson Q2U' or the 'ATR2100'. These microphones aren't that expensive – they're less than $100. But they make a world of difference to your audio quality. And good audio is a massive part of good video.

81) Distribution is key today in our noisy, noisy internet - Chad Pollitt

You can produce all the quality content that you like, but unless you have a distribution strategy, you're unlikely to be able to build a large audience.

Chad Pollitt from *Inpwrd.com* says: "I've been in this business for a long time. I can tell you that I remember a day when you could build it and they would come. You could hit publish and the search engines and social media sites would drive all the traffic you needed.

"But in today's day and age, there's so much content on the internet, it doesn't quite work that way for most businesses anymore. The average television ad executive spends five dollars on the distribution, promotion and amplification of their content for every dollar that they spend on creative.

"We need to rewire our brains and understand that we have to invest some serious distribution budget behind the content that we produce. We all know that interruptive advertising, such as display and banners tends to deliver miserable performance. That's what has given rise to influencer marketing and native advertising.

"Native advertising is the amplification and promotion of real content. I'm not talking about landing pages or product pages, I'm talking about real, top-of-funnel content that's helpful to a prospective audience – putting serious budget behind that.

> *"We need to put serious distribution budget behind the content that we produce."*
> **CHAD POLLITT**
> *@ChadPollitt*

"There's several ways that you can do this. For instance, you could go to individual native advertising networks or social media networks and use their systems. Or you can use a solution like our own, with an artificial intelligence layer that sits over 40 of these social media and native advertising networks, letting you scale amplification and manage everything from one place.

"One last thought... I'd say that we're starting to evolve from a click economy to an engagement economy. In years past it was normal for you to pay per thousand impressions. It was an impressions-based economy. Nowadays, most of the solutions are based on a click economy, but value is driven by engagement.

"This is a challenge for content marketers, because we want engagement with our content. We don't care about the click, because two thirds of those clicks often bounce quickly. We need to rewire our brains and understand that distribution and true engagement is critical today in our noisy, noisy internet."

82) Keep on promoting your best content - Zac Johnson

Following on from Chad's tip, should you be promoting all of your content or should you be quite selective in the content that you choose to promote? Zac Johnson from *Blogging.org* believes in selectivity.

> *"Create the best possible content and then continually reference it"*
> **ZAC JOHNSON**
> *@zacjohnson*

Zac says: "I've been in this game for 20 years now. Throughout that time I've found that there are two consistent things that marketers should focus on: branding and expertise.

"It is easy to focus on channels such as YouTube, social media and having your own blog. But you shouldn't negate spending time on how you're going to position yourself as an expert within your niche and what the best way of positioning that expertise to your target audience might be.

"You could achieve this through being interviewed on podcasts, writing guest blog posts on other sites or by running your own expert roundups on your own site. But you need to be creating value and then taking the time to promote that value.

"This also comes back to what some many other experts have touched on so far – so many marketers focus on the content, but not enough of them focus on promoting it. This is a big problem, because the internet has over a billion websites nowadays and the last thing we need is more content! This is why you should just be promoting your best content.

"Most marketers will publish a blog post, share it on social media and then forget about it. They might have spent a week or two writing an article, but only a minute promoting it. It's like they're burying their best content!

"What you need to do is to create the best possible content and then continually reference it, every time you're on a new podcast or guest blogging. As long as you're creating really great, evergreen content that's going to be resourceful for years to come, you should keep spending time promoting it. That's how you're going to eventually rank higher in the search results than your competitors – by building an authoritative piece of content that other experts continually refer to over time."

Chapter 7: Content Planning, Production & Promotion – summary

i)   Don't post on social media or publish content anywhere else unless you're sharing something valuable – respect your consumer's time

ii) Be relevant, concise and helpful with the content you produce

iii) Show up consistently for your audience, and focus on providing what they need

iv) Stop playing it too safe with your content

v) Go to *Alexa.com*, register for the free trial and use it as an opportunity to fill your content marketing calendar for the next six months

vi) Use Keyword Hero (*https://keyword-hero.com*) to get back the keyword data you thought you had lost and use this to power your content marketing

vii) Stop trying to match the word count of your competitors – your blog posts should be as long as they need to be

viii) The main difference between you and your competitor in a huge market is you – how can you incorporate more of your personality into your content?

ix) Your brand isn't what you say it is anymore, it's what consumers say it is – what stories are consumers sharing about your company by themselves?

x) Most marketers aren't putting in enough time to get world-class at content marketing – quantity leads to quality. The more you do, the better you get

xi) Make sure that your audio and video quality is good enough to stop consumers from getting frustrated and moving on to the next thing that catches their eye

xii) The average television ad executive spends five dollars on the distribution, promotion and amplification of their content for every dollar that they spend on creative – what is your content distribution budget?

xiii) Create the best possible content and then continually reference it, every time you're on a new podcast or guest blogging

8

SOCIAL MEDIA & REAL-TIME MARKETING

Although the previous chapter talked about how to proceed with planning your content marketing activities, unfortunately, as we'll discover over the next few tips, not all such opportunities can be planned.

83) Include real-time marketing as part of your strategy - David Meerman Scott

According to David Meerman Scott, marketing strategist and bestselling author of eleven books including *Fanocracy* and *The New Rules of Marketing and PR*, real-time marketing should be a very important part of your content marketing mix.

David says: "I'm really passionate about the idea of real-time marketing. What I've noticed is that so many marketers are marketing in 'campaign mode'. They plan ahead, they plan for next week, next month and next year. They plan their email marketing ahead of time. They've got all of their paid campaigns set up and ready to go and they pre-write all of their blog posts.

"The problem with planning everything ahead of time is that you're not prepared for what's happening right now, what's happening on Twitter and in the news cycle right now.

"Marketers are finally starting to recognise that real-time marketing is an essential component to marketing itself. There's such an opportunity around communicating in real-time, yet so few of us marketers are doing it.

"The problem with planning everything ahead of time is that you're not prepared for what's happening right now."
DAVID MEERMAN SCOTT
@dmscott

"In the old days, we didn't have the ability to do real-time marketing. In the old days, you had to do advertising – magazine, radio, television, newspaper and billboard advertising were all organized way before it actually took place. You create marketing now and it would be displayed in the future. But now, you have an opportunity to create it and then it's live, straight away. We're doing real-time marketing right now as we livestream while creating the content for Marketing Now, the book.

"I'm a huge fan of newsjacking, which is a form of real-time marketing. Newsjacking is when you understand the news cycle, and every news cycle breaks in exactly the same way. Every news cycle breaks, peaks, and then drops-off. When a news story is breaking, that's when reporters and editors are looking for experts to quote in their articles.

"When news stories are breaking, that's when journalists are active on social networks, perhaps around a hashtag for that particular news story. That's the moment where consumers are looking for products and services that are related to the news story and every day news stories break.

"As an example, a friend of mine called Mitch Jackson is a lawyer in Southern California. Mitch 'newsjacks' by publishing a legal take on breaking stories. He's poised to write a blog post at the exact moment that a story starts breaking, expanding on it, analysing what it means.

"Remember, Mitch is a lawyer, so he's eminently qualified to do that. When he does that, the media are looking for authorities to quote. If television stations are looking for experts to make sense of what's just happened, they're likely to call on Mitch, because he was one of the first people to write a blog post about the breaking story. Anybody can do this around their area of expertise.

"I use my smartphone or desktop computer to take advantage of this strategy, checking Google News every single day. Some days, depending on what's happening or what's likely to happen, I'll check my phone every hour. This gives me an opportunity to discover what's happening in the news. I can then write a real-time blog post on a related topic. I can post a YouTube video in real-time, I can tweet with the hashtag that everyone else is using, do a live stream – whatever it takes to take advantage of the opportunity."

84) Take the same approach that you'd take as a friend in your social media - Julia Bramble

The challenge with jumping on social media in real-time for brands can often be managing tone-of-voice effectively as well as trying to avoid words or phrases that don't match with your brand personality.

Julia Bramble from *BrambleBuzz.co.uk* says "We all know just how busy the internet can be. In the world of social media it's easy to lose people's attention and therefore lose the ability to grow relationships.

"What do most consumers look for on social media? They look for friends, to see what their friends are doing. Nowadays, marketers in businesses need to act more like a friend on social media. Acting like a friend means sharing the tips and information that your network of close contacts really need.

"Don't share just any old stuff, Place the emphasis on what your audience really needs. This may mean something that raises a smile. It could mean something that resonates. It may mean being empathetic. It certainly means following-up. It also means not expecting a target client to jump straight over to your website when you've only just met them!

"Being like a friend on social media means all of the things that you would naturally do as a human being, such as what you would talk about when you're out with your friends, perhaps even including telling a funny story about something that's gone wrong, because that's what friends are for.

> *"Nowadays, marketers in businesses need to act more like a friend on social media."*
> **JULIA BRAMBLE**
> *@JuliaBramble*

"The more businesses that can go out there and emulate being a friend to someone on social media – not only when they're marketing, but also during the whole customer life cycle – the better their results are going to be."

85) Put some sparkle into your social content - Katy Howell

For Katy Howell from *ImmediateFuture.co.uk*, making it personal on social media includes adding some sparkle! Katy says "My big marketing tip for you is to put the wiggle back into your social content!

"The past year or so has been fantastic for video-based brand activity. Video is having a phenomenal effect on everything else content-related that we do. However, even though it may not be easy or possible for you to produce video at the moment, it's still possible to put some movement into your content. This could be something as simple as an animated GIF.

"There are two rational reasons for doing this. First, you need to publish more 'thumb-stopping content' – content that makes your target audience stop and look in their mobile feed. You're much more likely to get someone to stop and check out your content if you deliver something that's moving – something that really stands out in a noisy social world.

"Publish more 'thumb stopping content' – content that makes your target audience stop and look in their mobile feed"
KATY HOWELL
@katyhowell

"Another reason why you should be doing this is that social network algorithms – for the most part – love moving content. This is particularly true for paid social media. You'll often find that paid social 'moving content' is prioritised over and above static imagery. Add that little bit more 'wiggle' to your content over the coming year!"

86) Start using Instagram to find new customers - Andrea D'Ottavio

Thanks to our previous tipster, Katy, you now know that you should be sharing animated content. But where exactly should you be sharing it? For Andrea D'Ottavio from *VagabondCEO.com*, if you're not on Instagram, you're probably missing out.

"You can engage with your competitors' audience on Instagram."
ANDREA D'OTTAVIO
@VagabondCEO

Andrea says: "My number one, actionable tip would be to start using Instagram heavily to find customers. Instagram is still very underestimated in terms of driving traffic and driving sales. Nowadays, content has become so very visual. Consumers love photos and videos. We're all staring at our mobile phones and looking at media from others and thinking about the ideal life that everybody else seems to be living!

"There's a lot that you can do on Instagram as a brand. For example, you can find customers just by looking at competitors. You can engage with your competitors' audience on Instagram. You can engage with people who tag themselves in very specific locations. And you can even – perhaps controversially – automate doing this with bots.

"My specific advice would be to use Shoppable Posts on Instagram Stories. If you have products and an online shop, you can sync your catalogue with Instagram and start posting your products right in front of your potential customers.

"By creating this kind of engagement on Instagram – without even spending a dollar – you can amplify your marketing efforts by getting a lot more relevant traffic to your website."

87) Get on the Instagram bandwagon - Laurie Wang

Someone else who's an advocate for turning more of your attention to Instagram is Laurie Wang from *LaurieWang.com*. Laurie says: "Instagram isn't just one of my favourite social media platforms – it's increasingly becoming the favourite platform for many others too.

> *"I expect to see a surge in the use of Instagram ads, particularly ads for Instagram Stories."*
> **LAURIE WANG**
> *@iamlauriewang*

"Instagram has seen a huge increase in usage across many age groups – especially in the 25-to-34-years-old bracket. I expect to see a surge in the use of Instagram ads, particularly ads for Instagram Stories.

"To emphasise how fast advertising on Instagram is gaining in popularity, in Q2 of 2018 alone the ad spend on Instagram jumped 177 percent, while the spend on Facebook 'only' increased by 40 percent.

"Instagram Stories is one of the most engaging elements of Instagram, with over 800 million people currently tuning in. It provides a great way for brands to showcase their behind-the-scenes content, to engage and connect with their audiences in a very authentic and personal way.

"I recommend using Instagram Stories daily for your brand accounts, but also as a marketer for your own personal accounts as well, to boosting the engagement of your account against the Instagram algorithm, gaining more exposure to people who aren't currently following you."

88) Use Pinterest! - Jeff Sieh

However, social media isn't all about Instagram and as Jeff Sieh's *ManlyPinterestTips.com* domain suggests, he believes that Pinterest should be high up on your list of where to publish and interact.

Jeff says: "Many marketers are not using Pinterest – such as bloggers and people who have products. The wonderful thing about Pinterest is that it has such an incredibly long shelf life for the content that you share. The shelf life of a Tweet is incredibly short. And as for Instagram and Facebook, the opportunity to reach a customer is gone as soon as they've scrolled past your content in their feed.

"The average shelf life of your images on Pinterest is around three months, so your content can be discovered for a long time on Pinterest. Did you know that the number one driver of social traffic to our articles on Social Media Examiner is Pinterest? More than Twitter, LinkedIn or Facebook!

"Pinterest is such a huge opportunity for bloggers. There are a lot of big companies not using the power of Pinterest at the moment. I would encourage you to try out Pinterest this year. It's actually a really easy platform to use.

"A lot of marketers don't use Pinterest because they struggle with producing long, portrait-style images – but it is really is worthwhile making the effort to do this and do it too a good standard.

"All you have to do is to incorporate image creation, publishing and sharing into your existing content production process. Just add that little sequence in to your process that you already have and you'll hardly notice that you're doing anything more.

"Once you see the value that Pinterest can bring you, you'll probably want to start testing software such as Tailwind (*tailwindapp.com*) which will help you to automate your Pinterest posting."

> *"The average shelf life of your images on Pinterest is around three months, so your content can be discovered for a long time on Pinterest."*
> **JEFF SIEH**
> *@jeffsieh*

Should every type of business that publishes blog posts with images in them be submitting those images to Pinterest, or is Pinterest just something that certain types of businesses should embrace?

Jeff says: "There's no reason not to be on Pinterest. I know a lot of people who think that Pinterest is just for women, but believe me, it's not. There are sports teams on there, there are tons of things on there for men. Many guys are receiving huge volumes of traffic from Pinterest. That's why I'm on it!"

89) Spend time with your prospects on a one-on-one basis, and assemble your team - Kristian Haanes

Kristian Haanes, Founder and CEO of *Webinara.com* would like to take this opportunity to remind you that your customers and prospects are real people and that you shouldn't get lost in the world of social media, hiding behind a computer!

Kristian says: "Planning is the one key thing that is going to define your success over the coming period. Both B2B and B2C consumers are over-saturated with offerings, meaning that you always have to ensure that your messaging is relevant and right.

"Even if you get your message right, it must be published in the right format and distributed through the right channel. It has to be timely, professional, precise and engaging. Less is often more. Spend more time on fewer things, but produce higher quality content and more relevant content.

"Even if you get your message right, it must be published in the right format and be distributed through the right channel."
KRISTIAN HAANES
@webinara

"My focus at the moment is on getting back to the basics, researching where my prospects are hanging out and doing what it takes to spend time with them.

"Join communities, run webinars and try to assume the thought leadership role. Personal branding is another key part to this. You run the webinars, you write the blog posts, you write the newsletters. If you just associate all of this great content with your company brand and your company brand only, you're missing out on an opportunity to personally relate with the consumer. If a consumer relates with you personally, your company will win too.

"Also, remember that marketing is too broad an area for you to be able to be an expert at everything. If your budget allows, assemble your team of experts to help you. You'll probably need a copywriter, a designer, a developer, an ad expert and an analyst. If you're not a good copywriter yourself, start with a copywriter."

90) Use social media to build relationships with thought leaders and potential future business partners - Mark Traphagen

As well as being a place to interact with potential customers, social media can also help you to build one-on-one relationships with potential business partners. This is something that Mark Traphagen, VP of Content Strategy for *Aimclear.com* has been doing.

Mark says: "Encouraging you to be more social and engaging on social media isn't a great tip by itself, even although engaging with your followers, prospects and potential customers is a good idea.

> *"Use social media to build relationships with potential partners, with people who are genuine influencers."*
> **MARK TRAPHAGEN**
> *@marktraphagen*

"What we've been doing is focusing a lot of productive effort – and seeing results – on making sure that we use social media to build relationships with potential partners, with people who are genuine influencers. People who are thought leaders in our space, but non-competitive. After the relationship is built, we expand and leverage those relationships, turning them into business opportunities.

"For example, when I meet somebody at a conference who was a great speaker and obviously has an audience in relation to the industry that I'm in, I make a point to meet them in person, to get their social media details, follow them and start engaging with them online. I try to be helpful, answering questions they might have, and perhaps providing them with data to assist them with their needs.

"As you're planting seeds out there at conferences and following-up on social media, the value can expand exponentially. We've had so many opportunities from these kinds of activities over the past year and we'll definitely be putting a lot more effort into it over the coming year.

"These efforts have provided me with opportunities to speak at conferences that I wasn't even aware of. It's led me to opportunities to co-produce content, to work on campaigns together and even to get recommended to new clients.

"This year, don't just promote on social media. Don't just engage with your followers (which you should be doing anyway). Specifically and strategically build relationships with people who could be your strategic partners in the future."

91) Get started with influencer marketing - Leah Buckingham-Warner

Mark's strategic relationship building with industry authorities brings us on to harnessing the power of influencer marketing. This is an area of marketing that Leah Buckingham-Warner from *LeahBuckingham.com* would advise you to incorporate into your activities, if you haven't done so already.

Leah says: "Influencer marketing isn't a new concept, but many companies are now devoting a lot more time to it. I think we're going to see many more companies participating in influencer marketing over the coming year.

"The reason for the growth in influencer marketing is that consumers are becoming more sceptical of brands and their marketing tactics. They're getting tired of seeing posts that are created purely to sell. They want to consume more trustworthy information.

"Building trust is crucial for brands. We all know that people trust people, and word-of-mouth has become more trustworthy than any form of advertising. Influencer marketing is word-of-mouth marketing for the digital age.

"As well as seeing a rise in the number of digital influencers, we're also seeing a rise in the number of micro-influencers, individuals who have grown their social media accounts in niche areas. These are the type of influencers who are now starting to dominate. Micro-influencers are the most engaging and the most relatable.

> *"Influencer marketing is word-of-mouth marketing for the digital age."*
> **LEAH BUCKINGHAM-WARNER**
> *@TheLeahBuck*

"Now is a great time for businesses of any size to get involved in influencer marketing, because there are so many great opportunities out there to grab!

Five steps to follow if you haven't started with influencer marketing

i)   Grow your followers and build your own community

"Keep your message consistent and show your personality. Let your audience get to know you, your business, your personality and what you're passionate about. You need to build your audience's trust in you at the same time as building their trust in your business brand.

ii) Make a list of the influencers you'd like to connect with

"Start with some small-to medium-sized social media influencer accounts and add in a few big ones that really inspire you. Focus on quality and relevance, not quantity. The key thing is to ensure is that their audiences closely match your desired target audience.

iii) Start building relationships with your target influencers

"In order for partnerships to work, don't view them as transactional. Think about them as long-term, not short-term. It's going to take a long time to build these relationships. There's various ways you can do it. You can provide value, share their content, reply to their posts, tag them in posts. Show them that you're endorsing them, because everyone likes their own ego being stroked every so often. Influencers are more likely to respond to you after you take the time to get noticed first. Quote your target influencers in your own blog posts and mention them when you share your post on social media, tagging them and sending them a message to say that you've featured them in your content. Then and only then – once you've built up a good enough relationship – reach out to them and contact them. See if they'd like to be interviewed by you, or see if they'd like to collaborate with you in some other way.

iv) Define your goals and how you will measure success

"If you're doing influencer marketing, are you looking for exposure, engagement, clicks or sales? Or perhaps something else? Whatever your goals are should help you decide who you should be collaborating with.

v)   Do your own research and be transparent

"If you're going to pay for collaboration, do your own research! Make sure you're transparent with your partnerships. And remember, just because your prospective partner may have a high number of followers, it doesn't necessarily mean that they'll deliver the results that you're looking for. We all know that there's many social media accounts out there with fake followers – just make sure you do your research and don't get caught in a trap."

92) We're moving towards the age of nano-influencers - Sneha Mittal Sachdeva

While Leah talked about the rise of micro-influencers, Sneha Mittal Sachdeva from *SuperSaaS.com* believes that influencers with even smaller audiences have huge potential.

"We're moving towards the age of nano-influencers, social media users with less than 1000 followers"
SNEHA MITTAL SACHDEVA
@supersaas

Sneha says: "We're moving towards the age of nano-influencers, social media users with less than 1000 followers, but with a very niche audience. These nano-influencers are regular people who are interested in promoting products that interest them and their followers, often at no fee.

"When you focus on promoting your products through nano-influencers at little or low budget, you can target an exceptionally tailored audience, while ensuring that your message is delivered authentically."

93) Leverage social proof to enrich your website - Mike Sadowski

You can utilise the potential of social media in several different ways. We've already talked about publishing more interesting, engaging content on your own channels. We then talked about leveraging the distribution and authority of 3rd party social media accounts through influencers. As you're about to learn, you can also use social media to enhance conversion rates on your own site.

Mike Sadowski, Founder at *Brand24.com* says: "My number one tip for the coming few months is for you to leverage social proof to enrich your website.

"Leverage social proof to enrich your website."
MIKE SADOWSKI
@brand24

"I'm seeing more and more companies take positive brand mentions collected from all over the web and displaying them on their website to boost conversions and build credibility. This shows clients or potential clients how the larger community perceives their brand.

"Think of it as next-generation testimonials – much more powerful than traditional testimonials, because they're clickable, you can see where the original content was published, which makes it much more authentic. This gives prospects the opportunity to engage with existing clients. It gives them the opportunity to check you out with a 3rd party.

"Embedding this form of social proof on your site is a really good way to boost your conversion rates from visitors to sign-ups."

94) Stop replying on free traffic from social media - it's time to embrace paid channels - Alisa Meredith

The fourth aspect of social media success that we're going to explore is paid social. You may have had a lot of organic social media success in the past. Even so, it's now time to embrace paid social media says Alisa Meredith from *TailwindApp.com*.

Alisa says: "I know a lot of marketers have become somewhat reliant on traffic from social media. However, we all know that organic social media traffic is decreasing and going away to a large extent. Now is the time to consider paid social media. I know it's hard to pay for something that we once got for free, but it's a reality – we need to start doing it.

"So many marketers aren't prepared for this. They don't have copy, imagery or a video that's worthwhile paying to promote. Not to say that their content isn't fantastic, but it's very, very difficult to make money on promoting content that hasn't been conscientiously planned as part of a funnel. If you haven't done so already, you really need to think about productizing your business in a way that's going to make paid advertising worthwhile.

"Pinterest advertising is quite powerful. It can be very affordable. If you're coming over from Facebook Advertising to Pinterest, the mechanics of it should be very easy to pick up. They're adding options such as age targeting and they already have some detailed location targeting.

"There's one little thing that Pinterest Ads has that nobody else has though and that's the ability to target people who have clicked on any pin that links to your website.

"If you pin something that links to my website and Jeff Sieh clicks on that pin, I can now target Jeff Sieh because he's clicked on your pin to my website. Also, Pinterest lets you capture your followers' audience, something that no other advertising platform allows you to do.

"I'm a big proponent of Pinterest Ads, but when you come over to Pinterest from another platform, it's important to realise the difference in the mindset of a 'pinner' compared with the mindset of users on other social networks.

"A pinner wants something positive, uplifting and approachable. If you have an article on '10 reasons why your diet failed last year', it's not going to do well on Pinterest. However, if you can reframe it into '5 reasons you are going to get your New Year's resolution accomplished this year', that would do better on Pinterest. Same content, different framing.

"Don't translate exactly what you're doing on Facebook to Pinterest... think about how pinners use the platform and what they want to see."
ALISA MEREDITH
@alisammeredith

"Don't copy precisely what you're doing with your Facebook Ads to Pinterest, especially if you're going to put serious money behind it. Think about how pinners use the platform and what they want to see. Inspire them and make it actionable."

95) Document your customer journey and organise your Facebook Ads around that - Mojca Žove

Staying on the subject of social media advertising, the 'biggest beast' at the moment is Facebook. So how do you begin to structure your Facebook advertising campaigns? Mojca Žove, owner of *SuperSpicyMedia.com* believes that you need to start with your customer journey.

Mojca says: "A couple of years ago it was easy to launch a profitable campaign on Facebook. But that's not the case anymore. Launching a 'conversion campaign' on Facebook isn't enough to ensure your success anymore, because a lot more businesses are advertising now than ever before. There are many more of your competitors advertising on Facebook than there used to be.

"If you truly want to increase your profits, if you want to launch a successful campaign – not just one advert, but a long-lasting campaign that will perform well in the long run, don't think of your campaigns as stand-alone entities, as many advertisers do. Connect them together in a funnel.

"Start by documenting your customer journey and organise your Facebook Advertising around that."
MOJCA ŽOVE
@mojcamars

"Developing your Facebook advertising funnel isn't really complicated. A lot of marketers think that it is, but I have a very special and easy way to figure out what your Facebook Advertising funnel is and how to implement it.

"Think of your Facebook Advertising funnel as representing the process of your a typical customer journey, where each step of that journey represents its own campaign. For example, if I'm selling an eBook and before someone purchases my eBook, he signs up for my email course and before that he visits my landing page, that's the funnel that I'm going to implement on Facebook Ads.

"As you sit down and carry out your advertising planning for the coming year, start by documenting your customer journey and organise your Facebook Advertising around that.

"Remember, the number one mistake that advertisers are making at the moment on Facebook is that they launch a purchase campaign and that's it. They think that because they're investing money in Facebook Ads, all they need to do is launch a campaign where prospects can purchase their product. That's not enough. If you only do that, you're not going to be able to scale the top of your funnel and you're not going to be able to grow your business.

"The quickest way that you can get going is to advertise a lead magnet. If you own software, try advertising a free trial to that software. Offer something of value, something that people can get for free. This way you're giving your audience an opportunity to get to know you and your business.

"Through this process you can demonstrate your authority in your space and your prospects will be able to see the quality of your work, your proposition or your software. This is the point where you can pitch them on buying something from you."

96) How to stand out with your Facebook Ads - Andrea Vahl

Following on from Katy Howell's advice to put some sparkle into your organic social content back in tip 85, Andrea Vahl from *AndreaVahl.com* recommends that you do something similar with your paid social media content.

Andrea says: "Focus your Facebook Ads around conversions. Keep an eye on your conversions and make sure that you're optimising your ads against that data.

"To optimise those conversion stats, stay on top of the media publishing options that Facebook offers. For instance, you can now use a 4:5 ratio for video on Facebook and there's a tall graphic that you can use which stands out much more in the news feed. These newer video and image sizes will be a little more eye-catching for your content consumers – and that's the key. Be more eye-catching than your competitors.

> *"Something that's user-generated can actually be more eye-catching and perform better than a professionally produced video"*
> **ANDREA VAHL**
> *@AndreaVahl*

"However, don't make the mistake of thinking that eye-catching means professionally produced. As Dennis Yu shared back in tip 24, something that's user-generated can actually be more eye-catching and perform better than a professionally produced video, because it looks like just a regular post."

97) Use your customer's stories as a cornerstone of your marketing message - Sam Mallikarjunan

To conclude this chapter, let's follow on from Mike Sadowski's use of social proof in tip 93 to further involve our customers in our content.

Sam Mallikarjunan, former marketing team lead at *BirdEye.com* and current Chief Revenue Officer at *Flock.com* says: "Marketers need to stop trying to do everything themselves. You've probably got a wonderful base of customers who are far more trusted by prospects than you. Start utilising the value that they can bring to your content.

"HubSpot does a survey every year asking this simple question: 'Which profession do you trust the most?' The most trusted tend to be teachers and doctors. Further down the results are politicians and lobbyists and then below them are marketing professionals!

"This means that if I said 'BirdEye's great' and BirdEye's paying me, you don't take that as seriously as if a customer of BirdEye told you that BirdEye was great.

"Don't sell a product based on price, sell a leading role in a story that your customers want to see become their reality."
SAM MALLIKARJUNAN
@Mallikarjunan

"So how can you make better use of your customers in your marketing? To begin with, reach out to them and ask them how satisfied they are. If they have a great story about what your product, service or solution did, how it impacted their life or how it impacted their work, collect that story and include it in your content.

"This is a great advantage for smaller companies and start-ups, because you don't have to have a huge marketing team to make this strategy a success. And the great thing is that it's also bringing balance to the universe – just because you have a big, sophisticated marketing team with lots of content, doesn't mean that you're going to be able to win the marketing game if your competitors' customers are saying better things about them than your customers are saying about your business.

"Listen to your customers and do the service piece too. Respond and engage. But after that, take it a step further and let those customer stories become your growth engine. Don't sell a product based on price, sell a leading role in a story that your customers want to see become their reality.

"Remember, let your customer take part in the content that you produce. Your website shouldn't be your marketing team talking to your future customers. It should be your current customers talking to your future customers. Let your customers create all that content for you and after that you're free to take more time to do the stuff that you love to do and that you're passionate about as an entrepreneur."

Chapter 8: Social Media & Real-Time Marketing – summary

i) When news stories are breaking, that's when journalists are active on social networks – use this opportunity to expand on the story and position yourself as the expert to call for a quote

ii) Act like a true friend on social media by sharing something that resonates or raises a smile – and be empathetic with your audience

iii) Put the 'wiggle' back into your social media content by using video or animated GIFs to encourage users to stop on your content in their feeds

iv) If you have products and an online shop, you can sync your catalogue with Instagram and start posting your products right in front of your potential customers

v) Instagram Stories is one of the most engaging elements of Instagram, with over 800 million people currently tuning in – how are you using Instagram Stories?

vi) If you currently blog, start incorporating publishing your blog post images on Pinterest into your content publishing plan

vii) Your message has to be timely, professional, precise, and engaging – spend more time on fewer things, but produce higher quality content, and more relevant content

viii) Don't just engage with your social media followers (which you should be doing anyway). Specifically and strategically build relationships with people who could be strategic partners for you in the future

ix) Focus on quality, not quantity when working with influencers – the key thing is to ensure that their audiences closely match your target audience

x) When you focus on promoting your products through nano-influencers at little or low budget, you can target an exceptionally tailored audience

xi) Take positive brand mentions, collected from all over the web, and display them on your website to boost conversions, building credibility

xii) Don't translate exactly what you're doing on Facebook to Pinterest, especially if you're going to put money behind it – think about how 'pinners' use their platform and what they want to see

xiii) Don't think of your Facebook advertising campaigns as stand-alone entities (as many advertisers do) – connect them together in a funnel

xiv) Don't mistake being eye-catching for being professionally produced – something that's user-generated can actually be more eye-catching and perform better than a professionally produced video, because it looks just like a regular post

xv) If your customers have a great story about what your product, service or solution did, how it impacted their life or how it impacted their work, collect that story and include it in your content

This takes us to the end of Marketing Now Part 2: Creative Success. Make sure that you've watched the workshop video on implementing this section of the book at *DavidBain.com/MarketingNow* before moving on to the next chapter.

PART 3:
PROMOTIONAL SUCCESS

9

THE FUTURE OF ADVERTISING & TARGETING

We touched upon social media advertising at the end of chapter eight, but online advertising is a vast and varied subject by itself and it's continually evolving. In this, the first chapter of 'Promotional Success', the third and final section of Marketing Now, we explore how marketing is changing and what that might mean for you and your business.

98) Learn how to work with the machines - Brad Geddes

Brad Geddes, Co-Founder of *AdAlysis.com* thinks that if you're still trying to run your advertising campaigns manually without leveraging automation and AI, it's likely that you are falling further and further behind the competition.

Brad says: "It's time to learn how to work with the machines. For so long it's been humans versus the machines. These days, from Bing Ads to Google Ads and systems like ours, you can set up and run your campaigns on autopilot. Some marketers accept this, but others still want to do everything manually themselves.

"Machines are great for doing a lot of background work. Humans are great for critical thinking abilities. The more that technology evolves, the more we have to evaluate our tolerance levels for how much we're willing to let the machines take over.

> *"Get started with machine learning by prioritising your primary goals. This will lead you to understand which experiments to do."*
> **BRAD GEDDES**
> *@bgtheory*

"We need to be confident in the ways that we're measuring the outcomes that the machines are delivering. Instead of blindly ignoring or accepting what machines are doing on our behalf, we should be judging their effectiveness as we run our experiments. We should also be learning how to work with the machines as opposed to against them and evaluating their performance critically.

"Get started with machine learning by prioritising your primary goals. This will lead you to understand what experiments to do – to discover what's helping and what's hurting. If you decide to accept and run with a machine's recommendation, make a note of when you did so and check back a week later to see if the results were good or bad.

"You need to get good at measuring a machine's performance. Everyone knows how to measure web traffic, but marketers don't tend to measure the effectiveness of machine learning and that's something that we should be doing now, as well as in the future."

99) Embrace the fact that machines can do bidding better than humans can - David Szetela

For David Szetela, owner and CEO of *FMBMedia.com*, the machines are already doing a better job at many aspects of paid advertising. David says: "I think it's about time for PPC campaign managers to finally admit to themselves and embrace the fact that machines can do bidding better than humans can.

> *"Machines can do bidding better than humans can."*
> **DAVID SZETELA**
> *@Szetela*

"I would encourage you to try Google's 'CPA targeted bidding'. This is where you ask Google to give you as many conversions as possible, or conversions at below a target CPA. You can also try 'Return on Ad Spend' targeted bidding, where you ask Google to provide you with as many sales as possible at or below a target return on ad spend.

"Another ad campaign strategy that Google offers is to target 'impression share' or target 'maximum impression share'. This is where you tell Google to give you as much top of the page impression share as you can possibly get. This may very well be a perfect bidding strategy for brand campaigns, when competing against competitors over select periods.

"Something else to consider is to target 'outranking share', allowing you to show your ads above your competitor's ads i.e.

allowing you to show your ads above your competitor' domain – really useful in competitive situations.

"However, be patient. This kind of software learns over a period of time, in the region of two weeks. I know a lot of clients and bosses who have short attention spans and can't possibly wait that long. You really have to hold them off until the software does its job.

"When you're making adjustments to your target CPA, or your target 'return on ad spend', only make an adjustment that is 10% or 15% different from the current one. After that, wait a week or two for the target CPA or 'return on ad spend' to stabilise, before making any further adjustment."

100) Build your campaigns with automation in mind - Aaron Levy

Aaron Levy who heads-up a team of 20 PPC experts at *EliteSEM.com* believes that the way to best make use of automation is to build your campaigns with the future in mind.

Aaron says: "My tip is to pause what you're currently doing, and let go of the past. With all the changes that Google and Bing are currently making to how their ad software operates, you need to make sure that your accounts are set up for the new reality.

"Stop trying to hold on to the past, trying to hold on to how Google used to do things. Stop looking back at year-over-year comparisons and look forward instead. As you start developing new campaigns, ideas and strategies, build them with the future in mind. Build them with automation in mind. It's now less about what we can do from a data perspective and more about how we as marketers can train the machines to do the right thing for us.

"As marketers we're really good strategists, but really bad calculators. Our role should be to move away from being really good button pushers, thinking about things like the fastest way to do an Excel test, on to thinking about how can we feed the right information into the robot and let it do the work for us.

"Stop trying to hold on to the past and trying to hold on to how Google used to do things."
AARON LEVY
@bigalittlea

"I often call myself the laziest search marketer. I work really hard at not having to work hard at all. I don't understand why marketers keep trying to do everything themselves. Make your next step to get rid of what you're bad at, focusing instead on what you're good at."

101) Make sure you're testing less-well-trodden opportunities & focus more on top-of-funnel - JD Prater

The previous three tips in this chapter have all looked at how rapidly Google and Bing are evolving their ad propositions. But what are some other top digital advertising opportunities available at the moment? JD Prater, *Quora Ads* Evangelist believes that it's a mistake for marketers to just to focus on the bigger guns.

JD says: "I think that we're going to see a greater focus on top-of-the-funnel over the coming year. We're going to see an expansion of different networks and more ad diversification as digital advertising prices increase.

"We can't keep on relying on Google and Facebook for traffic. We have to move beyond chasing algorithms of the most popular networks, where the only experimentation we do is trying different ad types on the same platform. Many marketers have tested all they can test on the big networks. If you've been in the paid search game for a while, you know that what you're doing now is primarily focusing on the bottom of the funnel.

"Of course you can embrace audience targeting, but this is not necessarily going to lead to significant growth. To get the growth that you're looking for, you might find that you have to turn to newer channels.

"Video ads on YouTube are going to get a lot more popular. LinkedIn is becoming hot. Look out for Pinterest and of course, don't forget about Quora too!

"You need to think about how your content marketing ties together with your top-of-the-funnel ad campaigns. All of this bleeds together because we're going to see advertisers spending more to promote their content in front of target audiences as a first-touch, top-of-funnel piece.

"We're seeing that already, almost 47% of all budgets around content are targeting top-of-the-funnel. How do we get more eyeballs on that content? I think that we'll see both platforms and users reduce their use of exact match search and move towards retargeting and audience targeting.

"If we're going to publish a piece of content that's highly-relevant to the user, we have to match the stage that users are at in the funnel to the content that's likely to resonate with them personally at that moment in time. Smarter targeting will bring more users into our funnel. We can then nurture them in a number of different ways that will probably include email and remarketing. This is what I think marketers should be focusing on at the moment.

"There are a lot of preconceptions that some marketers have about advertising on less popular channels. For instance, if I ask people whether they're advertising on Twitter, I often get the response 'No, my audience isn't on there.' I guarantee you they are! You just have to look at the hashtags being used. It's kind of funny that marketers have those preconceptions. Don't sleep on your audience!

> *"There are a lot of preconceptions that some marketers have about advertising on less popular channels."*
> **JD PRATER**
> *@jdprater*

"Perhaps these marketers have preconceptions about certain networks, but a lot of networks have reinvented themselves. Go and look at Pinterest, because Pinterest is no longer a social network. It's all about the user now. It's a very personal network. It's where you go to discover things.

"Make sure that you reassess advertising opportunities that you once dismissed with fresh eyes to see if your audience is there now. If the platform you're checking out offers the facility, set up a pixel and try to build a remarketing audience. Upload your email list to these networks and just see how many of your existing users are there."

102) Audience-based paid advertising - Damon Gochneaur

As JD touched upon in the previous tip, embracing audiences on paid platforms is an important aspect of how these networks work nowadays and how they'll continue to work over the coming few years. Damon Gochneaur, Founder of *AspiroAgency.com* believes that this is an approach that you need to master.

Damon says: "I've been a decade in the Google Ads game – and I don't know if I've ever been more excited! Because of recent changes, Google Ads is starting to feel like a brand new platform in a lot of ways, specifically because of their evolving audience-based approach.

"We've recently moved and migrated some of our largest spending and most aggressive and complex accounts to a completely different strategy.

"Instead of looking at tech-based keywords, look at who the audience is and where that audience is – and how to speak to and target that audience in a different way.

> *"Instead of looking at tech-based keywords, look at who the audience is and where that audience is"*
> **DAMON GOCHNEAUR**
> *@DamonGochneaur*

"Google is opening up the ways that you can use audience targeting, specifically on YouTube and Display. This lets you think about how you can warm-up audiences so that they have some brand awareness and brand affinity before they get to the non-brand, product search phase that you want to be well positioned for.

"Start to use an audience-based approach and leverage your first-party data. Too many businesses sit on goldmines of data without actually using it, such as big pools of CRM data and newsletter signups.

"There is also a great deal of actionable data that you can use in your paid campaigns, including the way that your email subscribers interact with your messages and the paths that your users take through your web pages. Too often, businesses just let that data die on the vine. Don't let that be the case for you!"

103) Understand your audiences - Christi Olson

Someone else who's keen on helping to ensure that you embrace and maximise the use of audience targeting is Christi Olson from *Bing Ads*.

Christi says: "We're currently seeing a big shift in the search landscape. For organic search, user intent is becoming just as important as keywords. For paid search, you can now layer audience targeting on top of your existing campaigns, helping you be much more pinpointed with your activities.

"What this means in practice for your paid search campaigns is that you need to start thinking about how your keywords are going to map to the different stages of your customer decision journey as well as the actions that consumers are taking on your site. This way, you'll be building out specific audiences, each associated with where they happen to be in your purchase funnel.

> *"User intent is becoming just as important as keywords."*
> **CHRISTI OLSON**
> *@ChristiJOlson*

"After you complete mapping how your keywords are going to align to the different stages of your customer decision journey as well as how they map to the actions that consumers are taking on your site, you should address:

i)   Your messaging
ii) The keywords that you're targeting at the end of your funnel, incorporating both negative and positive keywords

iii) Landing pages, based on the actions that users take on your site

iv) Your bid strategy

"It's going to get more complicated the further you go down this path, so it's important that you get the basics right to begin with. Layering audiences on top of your campaigns will help you to be much more targeted and personalised, so it's certainly worthwhile making the effort.

"The next area to think about is organic search – as I already briefly touched upon, organic search is moving towards intent. What this means in practice is that you need to start thinking about the user intent behind the keywords and phrases that you're using and targeting.

"This means, when you're writing or managing the production of content, you're not only targeting a set of keywords, but you're also targeting the actions that you're hoping to achieve on the back-end of your campaign as a result of satisfying the consumer."

104) Personalisation at scale - Purna Virji

As Christi mentioned in the previous tip, layering audiences on top of your campaigns can help you personalise the delivery of your messaging. Purna Virji, Senior Manager of Global Engagement at *Microsoft* would like to emphasise that personalisation can be achieved at scale.

Purna says: "You definitely need to start with segmenting and targeting your audiences, so that all of your copy and your ad messaging feels super-relevant to each and every one of your users.

"You have to do this for two reasons. Firstly, our expectations as consumers are changing so much. Something that was acceptable four or five years ago is often a big no-no now. Consumers compare engaging with a brand with the best experience they've ever had, not just with direct competitors. Make everything as smooth and as easy as possible for your audience.

"Also, businesses now have the tools to segment and target audiences effectively, so there should be no excuses for not doing it!

"Some marketers are overly focused on AI. A lot of digital marketers are talking about the advances in AI with the improved understanding of voice and images. All of that is really great, but we have to bring it right back to what the technology can do for your customer now.

"You should be saving some of your time by letting the machines take over some of the heavy lifting, such as the automation options on offer like bid management, the easy importing of data and reporting.

"Use your saved time to better understand your audiences, your different audience segments and motivations. This means that you'll be more able to craft the right message to the right person.

"Consumers compare engaging with a brand with the best experience they've ever had, not just with direct competitors."
PURNA VIRJI
@purnavirji

"However, an AI-powered development that you should be paying attention to right now is 'in-market audiences', available on both Google and Bing. Use this to make sure that you are showing your ads to a group of people who are actively in the market, ready to buy what you're offering. They may or may not have even heard of your brand, but you can still reach these audiences through these new targeting options.

"Something else that I'm excited about is what Microsoft is starting to offer through LinkedIn profile targeting. That's a new beta offering from Microsoft Ads, allowing you to target a lot more precisely, using data such as LinkedIn profile dimensions including company, job function, and industry. With all of these options at your fingertips, you can definitely hit personalisation at scale now and moving forward in your marketing activities."

105) Be more targeted with your marketing - Laura Crimmons

Of course, personalisation is something that can also be – and should be – applied to many other marketing channels on top of the ones that Purna highlighted in the previous tip. Laura Crimmons, Founder of *SilverthornAgency.com* is an advocate for marketers to be much more targeted in everything that they do.

"Local papers only want to feature local stories, so localising our stories will help to get them featured."
LAURA CRIMMONS
@lauracrimmons

Laura says: "We continually talk about the end-consumer, but we often forget about the middle audience of journalists that we sometimes have to go through in order to reach our end target consumer.

"With so much data and so many tools out there that can help us make sure that we are finding the right journalists and that we are reaching them in the right way, there's no longer an excuse as to why we're not doing that more effectively.

"This is something that AI is also being leveraged for. We can learn a lot from projects that are happening at the moment such as RADAR *(https://radarai.com/)* in the UK, which is working with the Press Association and the Associated Press, helping to revitalise regional and local newspapers.

"I'm using RADAR to take data that is publicly available, blending it with my crafted copy and then using RADAR's AI to insert appropriate local data, generating a localised news story for every regional newspaper around the UK. This is huge, and is helping to revitalise local press, which has been dying a slow death up until now.

"This kind of technology helps you to target and personalise your stories much more effectively than before. You should know that local papers only want to feature local stories, so localising stories will help you to get them featured. Do everything you can to personalise your stories and outreach in the future."

106) Use custom-intent audiences for YouTube - Joe Martinez

From personalising press releases to personalising YouTube advertising, our next tipster is Joe Martinez, Director of Client Strategy at *ClixMarketing.com*. Joe says: "I am a huge fan of advertising on YouTube and I'd suggest that you try 'custom intent audiences' for YouTube over the coming months.

"You may already be using in-market audiences for targeting in Google Ads. (Google provides a set of standard in-market audiences that lets you target prospects who are already actively looking for certain products or services. A lot of those are great, but using the default options aren't suitable for every industry.)

"I have a lot of clients that need something more specific – and you can get involved with this opportunity too by creating your own in-market audiences with 'custom intent audiences'. I find that this works really well.

"You can create your own 'in-market audiences' using keywords, URLs, or even apps that are part of Google's network – and that includes YouTube. Doing this on YouTube is where it gets really interesting and where I get giddy because it's under-utilised at the moment!

"We can now target users on YouTube who were searching for something specific on Google. How amazing is that? Do not tell me that intent only lives on the search network, because that's not true anymore!

"We can now target users on YouTube who were searching for something specific on Google."
JOE MARTINEZ
@MilwaukeePPC

"Get started by creating a list of broad-match keywords – this is where you should get as broad as possible. Everyone gets freaked out because it's giving Google too much control, we've seen the deterioration of match types already. But this is YouTube. This is awareness. You want to get in front of new users and expand your reach, building awareness for your products and services. Bear in mind that we still maintain control because we know that we're targeting prospects who are already searching for the terms that we've selected on Google.

"If you have certain sensitive keywords, such as if you work in the medical field and someone's typing in medical symptoms, you can't use those keywords. Same thing if you're selling guns or any products that you can't sell or promote on Google.com – that's not going to be allowed either. But unless you represent the type of business that isn't allowed to advertise on Google, you should be good to go.

"I recommend that you start building 'custom intent audiences' for your converting search terms and your converting keywords. Those are two different things – the keywords that you're targeting versus the keywords that your website visitors are using to find your site. Start with those two keyword baskets as your initial audiences.

"Then you can start to experiment. What's important to your business? Perhaps you can create audiences based off competitor names or names of your competitor's products? You can also create an audience based off your site search, i.e. the terms that visitors are searching for on your website.

"Keep on brainstorming and experimenting. You should be creating audiences based upon your top selling products, or the products that make you the most money. Start building your 'custom intent audiences' as soon as you can, being as specific as possible when you get started."

107) Investigate Amazon Advertising this year - Kirk Williams

To close off this chapter, let's follow on from what JD Prater shared in tip 101, about ensuring that you test less-well-trodden opportunities. Kirk Williams, owner of *ZatoMarketing.com* advises us to consider advertising on Amazon, whether or not you're selling products on Amazon.

Kirk says: "I know Amazon Advertising has been around for a while, but it seems like everyone, specifically Amazon, is looking at it as a great opportunity at the moment.

"Amazon Advertising is due to surpass Amazon Web Services in operating income by 2021, which is nuts if you think about it! AWS has been a significant part of Amazon's revenue for quite a while now and all of a sudden they're looking at ads passing AWS in revenue, which is a really big deal.

> *"In the past couple of months Amazon has grown to become the third largest advertising platform in the world."*
> **KIRK WILLIAMS**
> *@PPCKirk*

"In the past couple of months Amazon has grown to become the third largest advertising platform in the world. It's grown wildly over the past year and from what I see – we previously saw this with Facebook and Google – advertisers that get in early are likely to have an advantage."

Chapter 9: The Future of Advertising and Targeting – summary

i) Get started with machine learning by prioritising your primary goals. This will lead you to understand what experiments to do, to see what's helping and what's hurting

ii) Try Google's 'CPA targeted bidding'. This is where you ask Google to give you as many conversions as possible below a target CPA

iii) Stop trying to hold on to the past, trying to hold on to how Google used to do things. Stop looking back at year-over-year comparisons and look forward instead. As you start developing new campaigns, ideas and strategies, build them with the future in mind

iv) Reassess advertising opportunities that you haven't considered for a while with fresh eyes to see if your audience is there now

v) Start to use an audience-based approach, and leverage your first-party data while doing so

vi) When you're writing or managing the production of content, don't just target a set of keywords – target the actions that you're hoping to achieve on the back-end of your campaign

vii) Save time by letting the machines takes over some of the heavy lifting, such as the automation options on offer like bid management, the easy importing of data and reporting

viii) Do everything you can to personalise your stories and outreach

ix) Target users on YouTube who were searching for something specific on Google

x) Test Amazon Advertising

10

MESSAGING, CHATBOTS, AI & BLOCKCHAIN

From the future of advertising in chapter nine to the future of communications and data exchange in chapter ten, honing in on four key areas: messaging, chatbots, AI and the potential game changer called blockchain.

108) Messaging is becoming an essential modern communications channel - James Elias

One of the keys to reaching your customers is to engage with them on their terms, on their preferred platform. To communicate, that often means in a messaging app rather than through email. This is something that James Elias, ex-Google Marketing Director and current VP of Digital Experience at *Abcam.com* advises.

James says: "I'm particularly excited about the marketing potential of messaging platforms. I know this isn't necessarily a particularly new trend, but adoption is growing fast at the moment and I think we'll continue to see this accelerate over the coming year as more and more businesses test out what is still an embryonic and emerging channel.

"The shift to messaging is clear. 100 billion messages are sent daily around the world. 10 billion business-to-consumer messages are sent per month. A billion-plus people are on Facebook Messenger and WhatsApp. 53 percent of people claim they're more likely to shop with a business that they can message directly.

> *"53 percent of people claim they're more likely to shop with a business that they can message directly."*
> **JAMES ELIAS**
> *@abcam*

"When thinking about these stats, I also think about my own personal use of messaging, which seems to be taking up more and more of my digital life, for better or for worse! Messaging is an entry point to the web, to search and social platforms. It also supports a more conversational way of doing business, which is everything that marketers have ever aspired to.

"The direction of travel has been set by WeChat in China. They've integrated just about everything under the sun into their messaging platform! This includes content, payments, commerce and so much more. It's become the one app to rule them all.

"Businesses are now starting to understand the importance of engaging on messaging platforms. Switched-on businesses realise that messaging delivers a faster, more conversational shopping experience, helping consumers go from discovery to purchase in just a few message exchanges.

"As an example, check out Lego's buying bot. It's very slick, initially asking who you're buying for (in my case, my two-year-old son). It asks about your budget and your hobbies and then provides you with a bunch of options, then an option to buy, right within the platform. It's an amazing brand experience too. You can have a lot of fun with it. It leaves you with a lovely, warm feeling about Lego.

"Clearly, customer service is a growing part of messaging: automating and serving a customer's needs. KLM have a great chatbot which allows you to buy a flight, get your questions answered, get your boarding passes and discover your boarding gate.

"There are also a lot of new services that are being launched through chatbots – some really interesting ones such as Alcoholics Anonymous in Brazil, providing an anonymous chatbot to those in real need, at times when it's very hard for them to reach out to talk to others. You also have publishers and media players like TechCrunch and Spotify who use bots to curate, personalise and share content.

"If you're looking for your marketing to provide utility and new, delightful customer experiences, exactly where your customers are, look no further than messaging and messaging platforms as a way to do that.

"In terms of getting started, it's really important to be clear about the role of messaging and chatbots for your business. Should you offer a new buying experience, a customer service tool, a new service, or something else? I think you need to incorporate one or more of those options. Messaging isn't a one-off campaign, it's more of a strategic play – albeit one you can test your way into.

"Of course there are a bunch of agencies who can create your chatbot for you, but there are also companies like Spectrum (*https://spectrm.io/*) and Flow (*https://flowxo.com/*) who offer chatbot platforms, allowing you to create your own bot with no coding required. Hopefully this messaging introduction has inspired you to embrace the medium as a marketer if you haven't done so already!"

109) Select channels that have the highest engagement and the lowest competition - Larry Kim

As James touched upon, you need to be sure that you enter messaging for the right business reasons. Don't do so because it's a bright and shiny new toy. Do so because you've tested that your engagement metrics work better for you on messaging platforms than on other, comparable channels. That's the advice shared by Larry Kim, Founder of *MobileMonkey.com*. Larry starts "My tip's the same every year – you've got to mix up your channel strategy.

> *"There's a golden era of every channel. Embrace messaging now and get in before your competition does."*
> **LARRY KIM**
> *@larrykim*

"Typically in a company, your product and your messaging doesn't change that much over time. You just have to move from the platforms that have bad engagement and high competition, to the ones that have better engagement and lower competition.

"The area that I would be seriously looking into at the moment is messaging for businesses. Think of it as a replacement for email, where you can just message out your blog posts or event reminders. Instead of email, send your content through Messenger or WhatsApp, and have your customers engage directly through messaging. The open rates for messaging are around 70%, compared to about 5% on email. Click rates are about 20% on messaging compared to about 1% on email.

"These opportunities don't last forever. There's a golden era of every channel. Embrace messaging now and get in before your competition does. Less than 1% of companies are participating in messaging right now. Soon, APIs are coming out for messaging on Instagram and WhatsApp. It's a great opportunity to start now."

110) Chatbots are going to be employed in much greater volume - Kelly Noble Mirabella

As well as providing you with a different way to communicate with your prospects and customers, a lot of your messaging activities can be automated using the power of chatbots, and that's something that Kelly Noble Mirabella from *StellarMediaMarketing.com* is doing.

Kelly says: "I foresee that chatbots are going to be adopted in big numbers. Over the next year you're going to see more and more companies deploying chatbots. In 2020, about 80 percent of companies you see today on Facebook will have some form of chatbot.

"Because of the adoption of this technology – mostly on Facebook Messenger, but soon on Instagram, WhatsApp and everything else that Facebook own – you're going to see consumers completely embracing it as well. Instead of it being an intrusive thing, it will become a regular part of the ecosystem that we're in. If you want to succeed in the world of Facebook, you need to be looking at what Facebook Messenger chatbots can do for your business.

"When you're seeing drops in engagement, reach and traffic to your website or other platforms, possibly because of Facebook's organic algorithm changes, a Messenger bot can help to elevate those numbers and save your brand on Facebook.

> *"In 2020, about 80 percent of companies*
> *you see today on Facebook will have*
> *some form of chatbot"*
> **KELLY NOBLE MIRABELLA**
> *@Stellar247*

"Also, we're going to see more companies learn how to using messaging to get their target audiences outside of the Facebook ecosystem and start capturing their information, letting you own the customer data instead of relying on and putting all your eggs in the Facebook basket, which we've all been burnt by in the past!"

111) A chatbot can also be an aggressive sales tool - Mark Wright

Someone else who's actively deploying chatbots in his business and seeing great results from doing so is former UK Apprentice TV show winner and current CEO of digital marketing agency *Climb-Online.co.uk*, Mark Wright.

Mark says: "I believe that to be successful in business, you've got to be constantly growing it. The way to grow your business fast is thought the power of digital marketing.

"The best channel for me and my customers at the moment is chatbots. Chatbots are killing it for us at the moment! Chatbots are messaging tools on social media that respond to customers or potential customer queries through automated conversation. They essentially take the role of a customer service or sales representative in a business.

"Chatbots are going to be responsible for a cost saving of over £8 billion in staff wages by 2022. 85% of all customer service interactions will involve chatbots in the year 2020. This is going to be a big game changer!

"I was initially very pessimistic about how chatbots would work in my business, because I don't like the idea of machines taking over a human's job.

> *"Think about using chatbot technology as an aggressive sales tool as well as a customer service tool."*
> **MARK WRIGHT**
> *@Mark_E_Wright*

"However, I tried them in my business recently and currently we get over 27 leads a day from chatbots, reaching out to four companies a minute! When it reaches out, the chatbot pretends it's me. In our automated sales funnel we're getting around 27 to 30 leads a day, so I encourage you to think about using chatbot technology as an aggressive sales tool as well as a customer service tool.

"Some stats are saying that by 2020, the average consumer will have more conversations with bots than they have with their own spouse. I know the nerds are looking forward to that one!

"You've got to try to be the first one in your industry. You've got to be in it to win it. Here are some of the best tools to create your own chatbot now...

"The chatbot I'm using and finding best at the moment for Facebook is ManyChat (*https://manychat.com/*). That's working really well for me, engaging through Messenger. It's a free tool that you can get started with straight away.

"The best way to build your own chatbot to work on multiple platforms is to use HubSpot's chatbot builder, so you can implement that communications flow through your whole business. I've trialled every single chatbot builder, and the HubSpot one is really, really good. The other option that you have is to build a custom bot yourself.

"I use bots to outreach on LinkedIn, bots on Outlook, and of course bots on Facebook Messenger. Chatbots are going to significantly change the digital marketing game over the next year or so – and if used intelligently, and combined with the rest of your strategy, they're going to be very effective."

112) Conversational experience using AI - Aleyda Solis

Another marketer who is keen to blend the possibilities that new technologies offer with your present strategies is Aleyda Solis, International SEO Consultant, and Founder of *Orainti.com*. Aleyda says: "My number one actionable tip for this year is to start experimenting with with Google Actions (*https://developers.google.com/actions/*).

"In David's last book, Digital Marketing in 2017, I recommended that you start testing bots. I think that Google Actions is the evolution of that, because not only does it allow you to have bot-like conversations with your prospects, but it allows you to expand the conversational experience that you are able to provide through your website.

"This will allow you to compliment the information that you provide on your website, reaching a wider audience through the likes of Google Home. For implementation, use as service like Dialogflow (*https://dialogflow.com/*).

"There are templates that you can use in Google Docs to get you started, to generate things like quizzes and games. What you produce doesn't have to be very complicated, but you should start testing Google Actions to increase your understanding of what you might be able to do with conversational AI. Start to get a feel for the queries that you may receive and the actions that you may wish to deliver. This will help you to understand your customer's conversational behaviours.

"I've already tested Google Actions on my website 'Why My Web Traffic Dropped' (*https://www.whymywebtrafficdropped.com*), to test what users had learned from the website itself. This site is an opportunity for me to run a few experiments.

"Start testing Google Actions to increase your understanding of what you might be able to do with conversational AI"
ALEYDA SOLIS
@aleyda

"It's not that tricky to get started. Google provides a wealth of information on their developers' website, including a whole section for Actions. They provide a step-by-step system to create an Action with Google Docs templates, as well as with Dialogflow for those wishing to take it further."

113) Keep an eye on what big brands are doing with AI and learn from them - Sarah-Jayne Gratton

However, unlike the techno wiz Aleyda Solis, you don't have to be an artificial intelligence trailblazer to benefit from AI. Sarah-Jayne Gratton from *GrattonGirl.com* believes that there's a lot you can learn from what the bigger brands are doing first, before dipping your toes into the pool.

Sarah-Jayne says: "The power of AI is something that digital marketers everywhere need to be aware of. For example, Amazon... their AI determines what their customers buy next. i.e. their use of 'customers who bought this also bought this'.

"Netflix do something similar. Netflix's AI considers what viewers are watching, why they're watching what they're watching, and what they're likely to want to watch next.

"These big brands are able to use their data to make assumptions about the future behaviour of their customers. Marketers need to be aware of the way that predictive analytics can help you to understand and forecast consumer behaviour in most aspects of your business to take fuller advantage of AI.

> *"Marketers need to be aware of the way that predictive analytics can help you to understand and forecast consumer behaviour"*
> **SARAH-JAYNE GRATTON**
> *@grattongirl*

"You can see how rapidly things are evolving by looking at the number of virtual personal assistants that we all have these days. I'm surrounded by them. I have more virtual assistants than I do real people around me telling me what time it is, what to wear, what colours look good and what the weather's like! Marketers need to tap into the power of this because it speeds up processes, making everything more efficient – it's one of the ways that marketing is evolving."

114) Learn how blockchain will impact marketing - Jeremy Epstein

Another technology that's likely to have a monumental impact on the way that marketing done in the future is blockchain – and this is something that Jeremy Epstein from *NeverStopMarketing.com* would encourage you to start to understand.

Jeremy says: "My advice for marketers right now is to go and buy a CryptoKitty. CryptoKitties are the first example of a provably unique digital asset, secured by a blockchain. CryptoKitties is a game, where people can buy, sell, trade and breed unique digital cats.

"I believe that the eventual impact of blockchain for marketers in particular – and know this sounds crazy – is going to be as big, if not bigger than the Internet."
JEREMY EPSTEIN
@jer979

"I know that on the surface that this sounds totally ridiculous. I get it. But I would encourage all marketers to step back and remember the first time they heard about Twitter, Facebook, blogging or LinkedIn – and similarly dismissed those technologies, which have since become very important.

"I'm fully aware that the whole crypto sector is under a lot of scrutiny now and it has a lot of volatility and perception issues. But just like after the dot.com bust, back in the days when you could buy Amazon for $6 a share, it's important not to throw out the proverbial baby with the bathwater.

"I believe that the eventual impact of blockchain for marketers in particular – and know this sounds crazy – is going to be as big, if not bigger than the Internet. And obviously, the Internet is what has made modern marketing a thing.

"The reason why I think that this is important for marketers to start exploring right now, is that brands are always looking for new, unique, engaging ways to build relationships, creating experiences for their customers that can't be replicated easily and can't be copied by their competitors. It wouldn't surprise me at all if we see more traditional brands starting to experiment with these unique digital assets over the coming few months.

"It's still very, very early as a technology, but blockchain provides a number of marketing benefits. Firstly, direct to consumer relationships. Secondly, no intermediaries. You don't have the issue of having to worry about Facebook, Twitter or Google or any other big brand like cutting you off. There's none of that risk associated from entities like Facebook having an external situation that might force them to change their policies or access.

"One of the most likely avenues to get engaged in is blockchain-based games, because that's something that you can't do on other mediums. In addition to CryptoKitties, there's another game called CryptoStrikers which is about collecting your favourite football stars on virtual sports cards.

"Of course, there are a lot of technical hurdles at the moment. Getting a CryptoKitty is not easy by any stretch. It's probably going to take a savvy digital marketer a few hours to figure out how to get this all done, but the reason why I think it's worthwhile doing is that it helps you to understand an important part of the future of digital marketing. It's worthwhile getting your hands dirty and understanding how some of these technologies are likely to impact the tools that you're using or going to use.

"Find out about how some of these blockchain-based tools will benefit the customers that you're trying to serve. That way you'll be able to get a sense for what that future looks like before it starts to arrive in the mainstream.

"The way to get started is to go to *https://www.cryptokitties.co/*. This application single-handedly brought the Ethereum network to its knees last year, but has ushered in an entirely new wave of digital collectibles, which I think are going to be really important for marketers in the future.

"When this trend explodes, I don't know. But I feel pretty confident that it's going to happen. This means that if you're a digital marketer at the moment, it's worthwhile spending a couple of hours trying to understand it!"

Chapter 10: Messaging, Chatbots, AI & Blockchain – summary

i) If you're looking for your marketing to provide utility as well as new, delightful customer experiences, exactly where your customers are, look no further than messaging and messaging platforms as a way to do that

ii) There's a golden era of every channel – embrace messaging now and get in before your competition

iii) If you want to succeed in the world of Facebook, you need to be looking at Facebook Messenger chatbots for your business

iv) Think about using chatbot technology as an aggressive sales tool as well as a customer service tool

v)   Start testing Google Actions to increase your understanding of what you might be able to do with conversational AI

vi) Be aware of the way that predictive analytics can help you understand consumer behaviour

vii) Go and buy a CryptoKitty. CryptoKitties are the first example of a provably unique digital asset, secured by a blockchain – and blockchain is going to have a big impact on marketing in the future

11

DATA & ANALYTICS

How do you know if any marketing activity is effective unless you try to measure its impact from start to finish? Here in chapter 11, we look at how to improve the success of your marketing through the effective use of data and analytics.

115) Measure it - get good at analytics - Jeff Sauer

Jeff Sauer is Founder of *DataDrivenU.com* and believes that every marketer needs to get good at analytics. Jeff says: "Before you implement any marketing campaign, you need to ask yourself the question 'How am I going to measure this?'

"You need to have some kind of measurement plan. Make sure you decide on how you're going to measure the success or failure of your campaigns before you hit publish. Don't publish and then go to Google Analytics, trying to figure out the impact of your marketing activity. Set some kind of target for what you're trying to achieve beforehand.

"That's what I do in my business and that's what I say to most businesses that I consult with – don't just do marketing for the sake of marketing. Do marketing to achieve some kind of objective. Make sure that you can measure it beforehand. Then, do what any good business does: compare your estimates to your actuals and ask 'did we achieve what we were looking to achieve?'

> *"Don't just do marketing for the sake of marketing. Do marketing to achieve some kind of objective"*
> **JEFF SAUER**
> *@jeffsauer*

"To get started in Google Analytics, I always advise businesses to map out their objectives in a low-tech way to begin with. Try whiteboarding or creating some kind of Excel document that lists your marketing objectives. After that, find the tools to help to get you there.

"If you haven't thought much about this yet, I have a template at *Jeffalytics.com* that shows you how to fill in your objectives for any marketing programme."

116) Always measure the data when you experiment - iEva Zelča

Many marketers understand the importance of continually experimenting, trying new channels and tweaking customer journeys. However, iEva Zelča, CEO at *AccuRanker.com* would like to underline the importance of tracking the success of all of the experiments that you run.

iEva says, "Many things can be achieved by experimenting. When you experiment, set actionable goals. Decide on a set time period that you're going to try some new software for as well as how you intend to use it. Plus, make sure that you measure the result or the impact.

> *"When you experiment, set actionable goals."*
> **iEva Zelča**
> *@ievazelcha*

"For example, HubSpot has been working on optimising their content to see what works best and what doesn't work so well. They take note of the changes they make to their content and then track exactly what works and what doesn't.

"You should be experimenting too. But make sure that you measure the data to find out the change that has had the biggest impact. Start modifying your content and measure the impact of those changes."

117) Own your own data - Russell McAthy

One of the concerns that Russell McAthy, founder of *Cubed.ai* has is that many brands don't realise the importance of owning their own data. Russell says: "There are so many companies out there that rely on third parties to control their data. They rely on other technologies to capture and aggregate their data sets across all of the different channels that they work in, across all of the different interactions that they have with the customer.

"These technologies give brands new graphs and new data sets, however, the brands themselves often don't own the data. Whether you're working agency-side, consultancy-side, or directly for a brand, make sure that you own your own data. Go and get it. Store it yourselves. It's not expensive anymore. You can even have a third party store it on your behalf. But make sure that you own it.

> *"Whether you're working agency-side, consultancy-side, or directly for a brand, make sure that you own your own data."*
> **RUSSELL MCATHY**
> *@therustybear*

"I'm not just talking about your web analytics data. I'm talking about going into the APIs of the technologies that you already utilise. Go into AdWords. Go into Double Click. Go into the affiliate networks. Make sure that you truly understand the granularity of the data that you're utilising, because this means that you're understanding the decision-making behind it all. This helps you to validate what you're doing, enabling you to have the correct APIs and optimise the way that you work with your partners and your internal teams.

What is the biggest single thing that marketers measure that they shouldn't be wasting their time on?

"Most things!" says Russell. "For example, the amount of visits to a website doesn't matter. Bounce rate doesn't matter. Impression stats don't matter. All of those are metrics that are effectively utilised to sell something or to incentivize someone to do something. By-and-large, they all don't matter in the grand scheme of things.

"If I just take visits as an example... visits to calculate conversion rate is not a metric that should matter. This is because one person that comes back to the same page five times is a very different to a single visit from five different people.

"When brands care about how they capture data, they start to understand what is happening behind the scenes. It's like discovering the Wizard from the Wizard of Oz! This enables brands to focus on the things that truly matter."

118) Use Google Data Studio to help with your reporting - Samantha Noble

Once you have your data, what do you do with it? How do you make sense of it and what tools do you use to visualise your data? Someone with the answer to these questions is Samantha Noble from *BiddableMoments.com*. Samantha says: "My tip is to save yourself a lot of reporting time by making use of Google Data Studio (*https://datastudio.google.com*).

> *"You can save yourself a lot of reporting time by making use of Google Data Studio"*
> **SAMANTHA NOBLE**
> *@SamJaneNoble*

"If you're spending a lot of time putting together monotonous reports and you're pulling data out from Google Analytics, Facebook, Google Ads and other systems, you can automate that entire process by using Google Data Studio and making use of its different plugins. Pair it with Supermetrics (*https://supermetrics.com/*) and Google Sheets (*https://www.google.com/sheets*) to collate all of your data in one central location.

"We've done some work for a client recently where they were spending two to three days a month compiling reports for the board. These reports were huge, huge packs of information, but hardly anyone was reading through them. What we did was to take all of that data and combine it into a small, cut-down Data Studio report. This is the type of report that they're now using on an ongoing, weekly basis for each trading period. All they have is a series of sheets that they go through online, without even having to print anything out.

"All their analyst has to do on a weekly basis is to take ten minutes of their time, plugging some internal data into Google Sheets. Everything else is automated. They're saving such a huge amount of time every single month on day-to-day, monotonous reporting tasks. If reporting's a big part of what you do, you should be trying to do something similar too."

119) Don't trust any of your tools - Michael King

Just because your data comes directly from well-regarded tools, you shouldn't necessarily trust it. This is a message that Michael King, Founder of *iPullRank.com* is keen to share. Michael says: "I've found so many times that when our data is unreliable, it's because of the tools that we're using.

"Don't accept all of your data at face value"
MICHAEL KING
@iPullRank

"For instance, when you conduct a link crawl for SEO, a tool might tell you that you have 40,000 broken links. More often than not, the number's a lot higher than that. Take the time to download the links that the tool says are broken, crawl them and double-check to see how big the issue actually is before you move forward. There's a lot of opportunity in further verifying what the tools say rather than just taking all the data at face value straight away.

"In SEO, the challenge is that there's no technical standards. Tools don't adhere to the same thing and it's very difficult to look at one tool and then compare that data to the data available from another tool.

"Most marketers just accept things at face value because they assume that everything works! However, because my background is so technical, I've spent some time looking under the hood of all of these tools. I find that a lot of the time, things aren't what they say they are. Don't accept all of your data at face value!"

120) Respecting people's personal data and sending the right things to the right people - Courtney Sembler

As Russell McAthy touched upon in tip 117, although data from your analytics and advertising platforms may be your primary focus, there are other important sources of data that you should be aware of too. Courtney Sembler from *Academy.HubSpot.com* says "If you're an email marketer, you've recently had a busy time with GDPR. Moving forward, you need to be fully focused on creating and maintaining healthy email lists.

"You need to be fully focused on creating and maintaining healthy email lists."
COURTNEY SEMBLER
@CSembler

"From this moment forward, you need to be fully respecting people's data, making sure that the emails that you're sending and the audiences that you're selecting are as hyper-relevant as possible.

"Doubling-down on and focusing in on these areas will help you to deliver that personalised experience at scale – the correct way, making sure that you're sending the right information to the right people at the right time. Only those who want to receive your messaging should be receiving it."

121) The US audience should prepare for their version of GDPR - Chad Pollitt

GDPR may on the face of it be something that is only relevant to marketers and businesses within the European Union. However, that's not the case. Our next expert, Chad Pollitt from *Inpwrd.com* – in for his second tip after also featuring in tip number 81 – believes that similar legislation will be put in place in other countries around the world in the near future.

> *"The US is likely going to pass their version of GDPR soon."*
> **CHAD POLLITT**
> *@ChadPollitt*

Chad says: "For US-based readers, be ready and be prepared, because the US is likely going to pass their version of GDPR soon. Data privacy is coming to the US too. I know for a fact that we have politicians writing the legislation right now. I anticipate that over the coming months, for us here in the US, we're going to have to stay vigilant and be prepared for that."

122) Reduce your reliance on data - Alen Todorov

Closing up Chapter 11, Alen Todorov, Head of Growth & Marketing for *SEOmonitor.com* feels that there's so much data available to marketers nowadays, you should think twice before incorporating each source into your strategic decision-making.

Alen says: "I think that the main, actionable thing to do right now, as marketers, is to have a backup plan for when we have less data. This helps us to become more customer-centric.

"We have to be much more mindful about how we use customer data. If, sometimes, we are offered additional data about our customers from third party vendors, we should ask ourselves whether or not our customers would actually want us to acquire this additional personal data.

"Lower your appetite for consumer data, and think about whether you really need the personal data before using it."
ALEN TODOROV
@AlenTodorov

"Ethics will come more into play in relation to data management moving forward. We could be at a major turning point in the way that digital business is done. Consumers in the past didn't think about the extent of data that they were providing to the likes of Facebook. Having Facebook as a free service was more important to them than the personal information that they gave away. But consumers are now becoming much more savvy about the extent of the data that they are sharing. Businesses that understand this concern will be the businesses that consumers embrace tomorrow.

"I was looking at Google Trends recently. More and more consumers are researching words like 'retargeting'. That used to be a very specific marketing term. It wasn't something that the general population were aware of. Consumers used to be just aware that there were ads. But now, more and more consumers are becoming aware of how ads are targeting them. I push my fellow marketers to think about what their marketing plan would look like if they had less data, not more.

"Email marketing is more advanced on this matter. With email, businesses have to be explicit about what they're offering consumers. You have to be crystal clear about how you're going to use the customer's email address. Moving forward, your business is going to have to demonstrate that you have a distinct plan in place in order to manage your consumer's data, no matter the source. Otherwise, your company might be the next one in the news and not for positive reasons!

"To summarise, lower your appetite for consumer data and think about whether or not you really need the personal data that you're collecting before using it."

Chapter 11: Data & Analytics – summary

   i)   Make sure that you decide on how you're going to measure the success or failure of your campaigns before you hit publish

   ii)   When you experiment, set actionable goals. Decide on a specific time frame that you're going to try some new software for and how you intend to use it

   iii) Whether you're working agency-side, consultancy-side, or directly for a brand, make sure that you own your own data

   iv) Save yourself a lot of reporting time by making use of Google Data Studio

v) Most marketers just accept things at face value because they assume that everything works – don't accept all of your data at face value

vi) You need to respect your customers' and your prospects' data – make sure that the emails that you're sending and the audiences that you're selecting are hyper-relevant

vii) The US is likely going to pass their version of GDPR in the near future, so be prepared for when that happens

viii) Think about what your marketing plan would look like if you had less data, not more

12

PERSONAL DEVELOPMENT & PERSONAL SUCCESS

We've covered a lot of very specific advice over the previous 11 chapters. But apart from reading books like Marketing Now, how do you keep yourself up-to-speed with the technologies, strategies and personal skills that drive modern marketing success?

123) Stay up-to-date with ad platform technologies - Joel Bondorowsky

One of the key components to stay on top of is ad platform technology according to Joel Bondorowsky, Founder of boutique advertising agency *PPCDesigns.com*. Joel says: "I have found that Google has made tremendous changes to its ad platform in the past year – more than I've seen in the previous 10 years.

"There are all kinds of other related services and technologies that are changing. Privacy concerns, as well as consumer safety are shaping the way that PPC platforms, such as Google and Facebook handle and report on data. These concerns have also impacted compliance (i.e. what you advertise and how you advertise it.)

"From a technological standpoint, campaign targeting and bidding automation is constantly becoming more effective. Their goal is for you to succeed. It's a win-win situation. The better your PPC is, the higher your profits will be. The more money you make, the more you spend on their ad platform.

"You need to consider how you should be operating now, based on today's ad technology."
JOEL BONDOROWSKY
@liquidjoel

"Google recently published a page on their ad platform updates, which is amazing. (Check out *https://support.google.com/google-ads/announcements/9048695*). It's hard to believe how many new features that they've added or altered recently.

"Marketers tend to get stuck doing what they've always done, because it's always worked. It's pitiful that almost everybody keeps on doing what they've always done – even although technology continues to evolve. You need to consider how you should be operating now, based upon today's ad technology.

"Something that Google recently launched is called 'target impression share' – this feature is amazing if you want to make sure your ads are being shown all the time. They've released new metrics so that you can now see how your ads are performing based on whether they're above or below organic search results. This data helps you see if your CTRs (click-through rates) are working. Stay on top of all of these new ad platform features, because if you don't, you might get left behind."

124) Upskill, continuously - Jo Juliana Turnbull

Constant and never-ending improvement and testing out new software and new opportunities is something that Jo Juliana Turnbull from *SEOJoBlogs.com* embraces. Jo Juliana says: "My actionable tip is to upskill, continuously.

"For anyone managing a website, I recommend that you learn how to track the performance of your site using the tools inside Google Analytics.

> *"Learn how to track the performance of your site using the tools inside Google Analytics."*
> **JO JULIANA TURNBULL**
> *@SEOJoBlogs*

"There are many great Google courses available for free and those who complete them will receive a certification that is recognized in the industry. As well as Analytics, you should consider doing courses in AdWords, display advertising, mobile and shopping advertising.

"Something else that I would recommend is that you attend face-to-face Meetups and other offline events too – this lets you get actionable tips directly from and build relationships directly with people who are at the cutting edge of your industry.

"Whatever tools and platforms you work with on a regular basis, you should make sure that you know all the new features and that you are using each platform on a regular basis. This way you can easily monitor the performance of sites as well as providing great insight to your team and your clients.

"Platforms that I use on a regular basis and recommend include *Authoritas* for keyword research and tracking, *SEMrush* for providing web performance insight and *Screaming Frog* for crawling your site.

"If you are the only one using a platform or tool, train the rest of your team or have an account manager that works for the platform train your team on how to best harness its capabilities. It is important everyone sees the benefits of the platforms you have access to and how these platforms can provide value for your clients' websites.

"It's really important that you stay on top of what the best tools for your business are, understanding where your site traffic comes from, as well as how to measure success."

125) Embrace an opposite, complementary skill set - Jill Quick

According to Jill Quick, Co-Founder of *TheColoringInDepartment.com*, when upskilling, you shouldn't just be honing in on areas of your core competency.

Jill says: "We can be amazing at our job and have deep subject matter expertise, but without realising it or without having any intention, we can really mess something up at the other end of our business.

"We've all heard of the T-shaped marketer. I'd like to think that we need to bend a little bit more and embrace an opposite and a complementary skill set.

"I've trained a lot of people face-to-face recently. For example, I've trained a lot of fantastic web designers. However, a lot of them don't know SEO, so they caused loads of problems with the organic reach of their site. Some website designers don't understand good user experience. This means that although their site looks visually appealing, visitors struggle to navigate around it.

"As someone who loves analytics, I've had to take the time to understand user experience. I've had to learn visual thinking and storytelling so I can help to get the message across. For me, over the coming year I'm going to be learning more about other areas in marketing and not zoning-in on my core competency.

> *"You need to have a better understanding of what other marketers do."*
> **JILL QUICK**
> *@jillquick*

"Jono Alderson mentioned this back in tip number 2. Attend other meetings. Talk to other business users, agencies and supporters. You don't have to be a jack of all trades. You still need to be ace at what you do, but you need to have a better understanding of what other marketers do. There's no single job now. We all bleed into different areas, which means that we need to adapt our skillset. I fear that as marketers we've become too narrow-minded.

"This is a bit scary to start with. I've struggled with the visual storytelling side of things. That doesn't come naturally to me. But I think that it's made me a better marketer to study storytelling because I'm getting out of my comfort zone. Go and learn a little bit about what's going on outside of your bubble!"

126) Get your head out of the sand and start seeing what's going on in other marketing departments - Aiden Carroll

Embracing an opposite skillset is a message that is echoed by Jill's colleague, Aiden Carroll, fellow Co-Founder of *TheColoringInDepartment.com*. Aiden says: "I was having a conversation with a couple of very prominent search marketers the other day. I asked them what they were focusing on and they said that they were building remarketing lists for search advertising – building audiences around paid search predominantly.

> *"Get your head out of the sand over the coming year and start to look around at how other marketing roles can assist you with what you're doing, and vice versa."*
> **AIDEN CARROLL**
> *@Aiden__Carroll*

"One of them mentioned that they're using these audiences to target video advertising as well. I didn't think they were being serious at first! I asked them if they were trying to be funny, but of course, it turned out to be true.

"I then started chatting to them about Google Signals (the aggregated advertising product from Google that helps to tie remarketing and Google Analytics together, including advertising reporting features, demographics, interest reports and cross-device reporting).

"It just brought home to me the importance of becoming more multichannel in your approach. Becoming aware of where your 'blind' digital marketing spots are, how to better track across devices, capacities and functions. Being aware of how the capabilities of other channels are evolving will make your role so much more productive.

"Get your head out of the sand over the coming year and start to look around at how other marketing roles can assist you with what you're doing and vice versa."

127) Understand more about you, your colleagues and your customers - Ned Poulter

Ned Poulter, CEO and Founder of Manchester-based digital marketing consultancy *PoleStarDigital.com* thinks that you need to be learning from your colleagues as well as your customers. Ned says: "I see marketing as a very people-oriented business. I'm fascinated by people every time I travel to a different country. I find myself culturally observing people! This genuine interest in people is key to being an effective modern marketer, but also an effective business person and human being.

> *"Marketing ultimately is all about great communication."*
> **NED POULTER**
> *@NedPoulter*

"To begin with though, I would recommend that you focus more on understanding more about yourself – because it all starts with you. You may be familiar with Myers-Briggs and other personality profiling tools such as 16Personalities (*https://www.16personalities.com/*). Get to know your personality type.

"At my agency we've been using a similar tool called Lumina Spark (*https://luminalearning.com/products/lumina-spark*), which provides you with a radial diagram. I much prefer this to Myers-Briggs personality profiling, because Lumina displays the complexities in your make-up.

"Lumina Spark says that you can have the majority of your traits from one side of the circle, but you can also have traits from the other side as well, resulting in a what's called a splash mandala, providing a radial graph of who you are. It's really insightful, allowing you to understand more about yourself, which is hugely rewarding and applicable to lots of different environments.

"Then, after learning more about your natural traits, it's time to learn more about your team. And perhaps your clients and other key stakeholders as well. Because if you understand who they are and what makes them who they are, you can better communicate with them. Marketing ultimately is all about great communication."

128) Build your personal brand - Joe Apfelbaum

Another man who sees the importance of investing in you is Joe Apfelbaum, CEO of *AjaxUnion.com*, a B2B digital marketing agency based in Brooklyn, New York. When asked about his one piece of actionable advice, Joe said: "It's all about the personal brand.

"It used to be that business owners hid behind their company. But now, consumers are spending hours every day on social media. 96% of the stuff that they're looking at is from other individuals – not business brands. This means that if you're not taking the personal brands of your employees seriously, you're missing out on a lot of potential attention.

"You have to train your employees on how to be better at talking about your brand, creating asset libraries and sharing things with their circles of influence. LinkedIn has over 500 million people on it and 99% of those people are not posting anything! Most of your employees are not sharing anything, yet 40% of LinkedIn users are logging-in every single day.

"The reason that your employees are not sharing anything is because they don't have a plan, they don't have a strategy for their own personal brand. Do you have a content calendar for your own personal brand? You as a marketer might have that, but if I ask most CEOs, entrepreneurs, sales or marketing professionals, they don't have a content calendar for their own personal brand.

"This year, get serious about your own personal brand. Create a personal content calendar and an asset library. Get serious about your social media efforts and the social media efforts of the people around you. That's how you're going to take your business and your life to the next level!"

"This year, get serious about your own personal brand. Create a content calendar and create an asset library."
JOE APFELBAUM
@joeapfelbaum

How does Joe recommend that you get started?

"Step number one is to understand what your goals are as an individual, as well as your company goals. Once you understand your goals and you understand your target market – most people don't think of their target market – but do you have a target market, your ideal customer. Once you understand your target market, then you need to create messaging that resonates with the people that you want to do business with as well as the people that you like and enjoy spending time with.

"Most marketers don't think about creating messaging for their target market. They're just creating messaging for the world. They don't think about the different stages in the funnel. Most marketers aren't thinking about top-of-the-funnel education-based marketing, versus middle-of-the-funnel trust-based marketing, versus bottom of the funnel, persuade-to-buy marketing. Think about your goals, your target and your message.

"If you check out my LinkedIn profile (*https://www.linkedin.com/in/joeapfelbaum/*), I have a free webinar that goes through what I've suggested, specifically sharing what you need to do in order to have a better personal brand that has the right mix between business and personal.

"People want to get to know you. They don't care about what you do. Sure, you're going to be sharing about what you do as part of it, but your audience wants to know about your personal goals, your aspirations and your hobbies – the things that make you unique. Humans don't want to do business with brands. They want to do business with other humans."

129) 3 things to enhance your personal brand - Alex Tachalova

Someone else who's a big fan of you building your personal brand is Alex Tachalova, Founder of *DigitalOlympus.net*. Alex echoes Joe's advice, saying: "Start investing in your personal brand as soon as you can. It doesn't matter whether you're a consultant or you work in-house, it will always be beneficial to enhance your personal brand.

"If you're wondering where to start, pitch yourself as a guest poster to smaller industry blogs. I wrote a big post on Search Engine Journal that features 20 digital marketing blogs that accept guest posts, so if you're a marketer looking to write guest posts, that's a good place to start.

"As Jo Juliana Turnbull touched upon in tip 124, the next thing that I recommend is to search for physical meet-ups that are happening near you. Just go to *MeetUp.com*, search there and start building real face-to-face relationships with people in your industry.

> *"Start investing your personal brand*
> *as soon as you can."*
> **ALEX TACHALOVA**
> *@AlexTachalova*

"Lastly, you need to be active on social media. Facebook Groups are a great place to be at the moment. I was recently invited to speak at an event, just because I am an active member of a Facebook Group – and relevant groups are easy to find through a keyword search on Facebook.

"Those are 3 actionable things that you can be doing right now to start enhancing your personal brand."

130) Find that thing that really motivates you, where you have the most fun - Joel Comm

According to our next tipster, if you're focusing on building your personal brand, you should be building it around something that really motivates you. Joel Comm from *JoelComm.com* says: "I tend to take a philosophical approach to marketing in general.

"There's a lot of talk out there about hustling and grinding your way through to success. I just want to remind marketers that you are going to have your greatest success when you're in your sweet spot. Your sweet spot is not the number of hours that you work. It's not about staying late or getting up early, or working on the weekends. It's about doing that thing that really drives and motivates you and where you are having the most fun.

"I've reverse-engineered my successes over the past 24 years. All of the times that I followed the advice of hustling and grinding and nose to the grindstone, those were the times that at best, I've had moderate success – if any success at all.

> *"You are going to have your greatest success when you are in your sweet spot."*
> **JOEL COMM**
> *@joelcomm*

"My 'home runs' have been the times with the least amount of effort. I know that goes contrary to what a lot of people teach, but I've discovered this to be true again and again. Follow your curiosity, be willing to take risks – and then trust the process. You will discover that you will not only have your greatest success in business, but you will have your greatest fulfilment in life."

131) A formula doesn't always work: focus on the things that excite you as well - and go and be your audience - Lexi Mills

Lexi Mills from *LexiMills.net* has similar thoughts to Joel. Lexi is President of the Future of Search Foundation and CEO of *Shift6*. She says: "We need to go back to some of the core basics. If you don't care about the thing you're creating and promoting, you're never going to make great progress.

"On reflection, all my best campaigns have come because I just told everyone about it because I was excited. I think that it's very easy for us to try and formulate how to create a marketing campaign, but that hasn't worked as well for me.

"If you don't know your audience or your sector, it's going to show in the quality of the content that you publish and the PR SEO results. My recommendation is to go and be your audience. We never work on any site that we haven't used or purchased from before we go into an initial client meeting – neither should you.

"Go and be your audience. We never work on any site that we haven't used or purchased from before we go into an initial client meeting – neither should you."
LEXI MILLS
@leximills

"It should so simple, but far too many agency marketers don't do this. How can you go into a meeting with a clothing brand and not have used their website? Who doesn't want to buy clothes that are tax-deductible!

"Seer Interactive are very good at this. They have teams who have bought white walking sticks and walked around and experienced what it's like to be blind. Only when you do something like that can you start to understand what it's like for a blind person to use a website. Walk a mile in your customer's shoes. That will lead you to creating more meaningful, impactful campaigns."

132) When you strike gold, leverage it - Mat Siltala

When you find something that excites you and drives significant profits, leverage it for all its worth! This is something that the President and Founder of *AvalaunchMedia.com*, Mat Siltala recommends. Mat says: "I would say that there's no single digital marketing channel that should be your sole focus for any product or service. But if you find something that works really well, stick with it!

"For example, my agency is well-known for visual content. Visual content has worked really well for us, so we continue to refine and improve that particular service. Sure, we have to keep an eye on diversification, but you need to ensure that you're the best at delivering your speciality.

"Continually test other channels to see if you can come up with a traffic source that beats what you've already got."
MAT SILTALA
@Matt_Siltala

"However, make sure that you continually keep an eye out on whether or not your specialty is as impactful as it used to be, not necessarily through any fault of your own. For example, SEO isn't as easy or reliable as it used to be for bringing in free traffic. You need to be involved with paid search and social ads to compliment SEO these days.

"The key is to track everything. Track your efforts, track your ROI and when you strike gold, leverage it as much as you can.

"Don't forget that things can change. As Larry Kim highlighted in tip 109, make sure that you continually test other channels to see if you can come up with a traffic source that beats what you're already doing.

"Although my agency has done really well with visual content, if we were just producing the same type of content now that we used to produce 10 years ago, we wouldn't have survived this long."

133) Don't get distracted by 'sexy' things - focus on the fundamentals - Krista Neher

Although Joe Comm recommends that you find things that really motivate you; and Lexi Mills recommends that you focus on things that excite you, you need to counter that enthusiasm by not getting too distracted by 'squirrel syndrome'. Krista Neher, CEO of *BootcampDigital.com* says: "Over the past few years we've found it too easy to be distracted by shiny new objects.

"When you step back and look at what is actually driving ROI for your business, it's usually a handful of things and it's often the stuff that you've been doing for a long time. Spending your time and your effort in doing those things better is going to give you the return on the investment that you need.

> *"It's often easy for marketers to get distracted by newer technologies"*
> **KRISTA NEHER**
> *@ KristaNeher*

"I'm working with a billion dollar company at the moment. When we look at where their digital marketing time and effort goes, a lot of it is on things like chatbots. Nobody in the organisation has been trying to improve their search ads in the past year! Search ads are a proven strategy. If you can improve the effectiveness of your search ads, I guarantee you'll get ROI from that.

"It's often easy for marketers to get distracted by newer technologies – and it's easy to forget the stuff that really matters. Avoid distractions. Think about the core things that are going to really grow your business and deliver the return on investment that you're looking for. This is probably the least sexy thing to say, but if you focus on the things that matter, that's where most of your results are going to come from."

So what according to Krista are the other pillars of long-term digital success?

"For most businesses, content, media and your website are the three cornerstones that are going to drive your results. Yet, what I see on Facebook is everyone wanting a chatbot when their content has low relevancy scores. If your relevancy score is one, two or three, this means that you're paying a lot more than you should for your advertising – and it means that nobody likes your stuff. It has no impact. Your target audience just scrolls way past it.

> *"Commit to being the best at what you do,*
> *which is what sets you apart from*
> *other marketers."*
> **JEFF GILLS**
> ***@digitmarx***

"It's hard to make good content. It's much easier in some ways to launch a chatbot or embrace another new technology. I think we have enough proven marketing activities that work now. But there are all these fun, sexy things that we want to try to do and it's a big distraction. Your big focus right now should be on the fundamentals, on what really matters to drive business impact."

134) Commit - Jeff Gills

Last but not least, don't just try to do something the one time (such as writing copy for your website) and then forget about it. Just as business propositions evolve, the expectations of your customers evolve too. Unless you're keeping up with both, your lack of commitment will cost you – sooner rather than later.

As Jeff Gills from *DigitMarx* says: "You commit first to your business, starting-up and getting that first client. You then commit to being a faithful servant to your client. However, you can also commit to being the best at what you do, which is what sets you apart from other marketers.

"But you don't become the best at what you do without making and keeping multiple commitments along the way. Commit to begin. Commit to serve. Then commit to being the best."

Chapter 12: Personal Development & Personal Success – summary

i)   It's pitiful that almost everybody keeps on doing what they've always done – even though technology continues to evolve. You need to consider how you should be operating now, based on today's marketing technology

ii) Practice constant and never-ending improvement, testing out new software and new opportunities. Start off by up-skilling in Google Analytics

iii) In the future, you will still need to be ace at what you do, but you will need to have a better understanding of what other marketers do

iv) Get your head out of the sand over the coming year and start to look around at how other marketing roles can assist you with what you're doing and vice versa

v)   Focus on understanding more about yourself, your team and other stakeholders to become a much better communicator and therefore, a much better marketer

vi) This year, get serious about your own personal brand. Create a content calendar and an asset library. Get serious about your social media efforts and the social media efforts of the people around you.

vii) Start investing in your personal brand as soon as you can – and if you're wondering where to start, start by pitching yourself as a guest poster to smaller industry blogs

viii) You are going to have your greatest success when you are in your sweet spot – doing that thing that really drives and motivates you, and where you have the most fun

ix) If you don't know your audience or your sector, it's going to show in the quality of the content and the PR that you publish – go and be your audience before you serve them

x) Continually test other channels to see if you can come up with a traffic source that beats what you've already got

xi) There are all these fun, sexy things that we want to try and do, and it's a big distraction. Your big focus now should be on the fundamentals, and on what really matters to drive business impact

xii) Commit to being the best at what you do, which is what sets you apart from other marketers

Now is the time to check out the third of our three implementation workshop videos over at *DavidBain.com/MarketingNow*.

CLOSING THOUGHTS

In my last book, 'Digital Marketing in 2017' I talked about the importance of becoming a good 'T' shaped marketer. But as Jill Quick touched upon in tip 125, that by itself doesn't seem to be enough to maintain your position as an outstanding marketer nowadays.

In my opening thoughts I mused over whether or not digital marketing has now simply become 'marketing', encompassing an increased awareness of customer journeys and more traditional marketing models that still work in the digital world.

But even if traditional and digital marketers marry their philosophies, they're still not achieving as much as they might do if they worked closely with other areas in the business too.

To be a super-successful marketer now and in the future, you need to understand how you can work more closely with sales and customer service – and you need to understand and help to improve the business model of the business that you work in. It all blends together now. Just about anything that happens in a business impacts marketing, whether you like it or not.

Of course, there will be elements of this book that aren't appropriate for you to focus on right now, but they may be right for you and your business in the near future. There will be pieces of advice that may never be right for you personally. Even so, retaining that broad awareness of what's important in marketing now will leave you with a firmer platform from which to proceed.

Every marketer will be different in terms of the subjects that require further exploration initially. For me it's the following ten tips that shone through the most and that I intent to follow-up with straight away:

Tip 2 by Jono Alderson: "Essentially, the secret to success is to have a fast, easily usable, technically flawless website with excellent content that truly helps your users." Sounds simple and perhaps even uninspiring, but this is where many gains can be made. What's the point in optimizing your digital ads if your user experience is second rate?

Tip 7 by Kevan Lee: "We take a lot of inspiration from the folks at HubSpot and their flywheel exercise. It goes like this: You create the initial flywheel by identifying the core ways you attract customers; the ways you engage customers and the ways you delight customers." This is a wonderful new way to map the customer funnel, resulting in a much better appreciation of how each stage impacts your future success.

Tip 18 by Greg Gifford: "Google My Business is the new homepage of your website if you're a local business. All the things that the customer used to go to your website for – such as directions, a little bit more about you as a brand, testimonials, your phone number, pictures of your business – this all now happens on Google's Knowledge Panel." If your business has a physical address, you're certainly missing out on a significant amount of digital presence by not taking advantage of everything inside Google My Business.

Tip 22 by Gavin Bell: "Create video content and use Facebook Ads to promote your video content, driving people further into your funnel." Gavin's approach reminded me of Simon Sinek's 'Start With Why' book. Too many marketers try to sell directly to a cold prospect on Facebook, incorrectly concluding that the channel doesn't work for their business. Don't make the same mistake – create a multi-stepped approach to advertising on Facebook.

Tip 54 by Emeric Ernoult: "Companies that focus on monetization and retention, as well as just acquisition, are growing three times faster than companies that just focus on acquisition – what are your monetization and retention strategies?" This underlines the importance of marketers understanding business models and other areas in the businesses as well as the marketing discipline itself in order to maximize the positive impact of their endeavors.

Tip 60 by Andrew and Pete: "Follow the 90-10 rule, where you spend 90% of your marketing efforts doing one thing remarkably well and 10% of your marketing efforts experimenting with everything else". I love this tip because it breaks the 'be everywhere' mentality that so many marketers end up chasing their tails with. Native interaction and the quality of your content is what consumers appreciate.

Tip 81 by Chad Pollitt: "Create the best possible content and then continually reference it, every time you're on a new podcast or do a guest blog." To me (alongside Jimmy Daly's tip number 64 to create a content library), this is much better, more strategic content marketing approach than the majority of marketers take. Structure and fill your content library before moving on to continually promoting your best content.

Tip 100 by Aaron Levy: "I often call myself the laziest search marketer. I work really hard at not having to work hard at all. I don't understand why marketers keep trying to do everything themselves. Make your next step to get rid of what you're bad at and focus on what you're good at." This is advice that I need to listen to myself as I'm often guilty of doing too much on my own, not outsourcing enough.

Tip 106 by Joe Martinez: "Try 'custom intent audiences' for YouTube over the coming months, using your target keyword phrases." I love hearing about newer paid advertising opportunities that are currently under-utilized and can reach a very specific target audience. Something else that could sit alongside this tip is JD Prater's advice to try Quora Ads from tip 101.

Tip 130 by Joel Comm: "You are going to have your greatest success when you are in your sweet spot – doing that thing that really drives and motivates you and where you have the most fun." Again, thinking about how I've worked in the past, I've often grafted hard without following my passion. Great advice Joel!

I really want to emphasise that I'm not necessarily recommending that you focus on the above 10 tips as well, I'm merely sharing the advice that resonated with me the most and encouraging you to select and further explore the tips that happen to be right for you and your business at this moment in time.

What stood out for you? What tip hit home the most? I'd be delighted if you'd share your thoughts with me on Twitter (*https://twitter.com/DavidBain*) or on LinkedIn (*https://www.linkedin.com/in/davidbain/*), using the hashtag #MarketingNow.

And remember – if you haven't done so already – to sign up for free access to recordings of the Marketing Now implementation workshops at *DavidBain.com/MarketingNow* to help you implement everything that has been shared over course of this book. Until we meet again, or meet face-to-face for the first time, adios!

Printed in Great Britain
by Amazon

33454570R00153